T3XTURE

nO.5

2021-22

REPOSE + ENERGY

Layout and Design:
Randy Sovich
Front Cover Art:
Joseph Mullan

ISSN 2380-4696

architecture, landscape, the city and the house through texts, poetry, painting, drawing, photography, design and constructions.

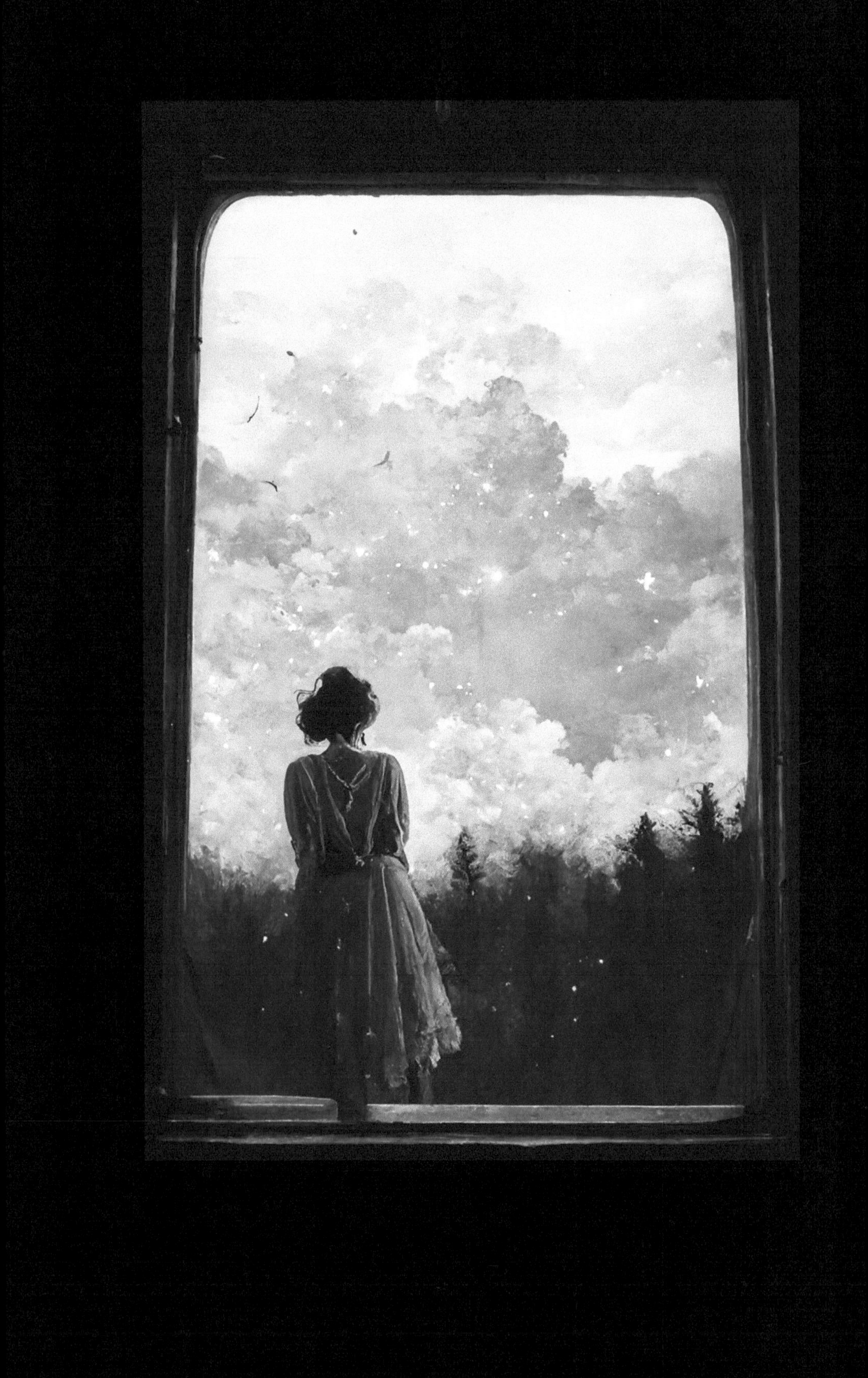

THOUGHTS ON REPOSE +ENERGY

"That moment, that wonderful feeling of excitement, why does it always pass? Even when you know it's special right then, and there, it still ends. Why can't we stay in that moment, that feeling? Why can't it last forever like we wish it could?"[1]

While we cannot actually stop time, as May does in the series, *Tales from the Loop*, we may have experienced a special moment we wished to save or savor—a moment with a loved one or an instant of feeling safe or at peace. One may have felt it watching the stars in a boat on a lake. Standing in the Pantheon. Listening to a song in a park on the Fourth of July.

Some people believe that architecture can freeze moments in space. Goethe, for example, famously referred to architecture as "frozen music." His colleague Shilling explained that for Goethe, "a beautiful building is in fact nothing more than music perceived with the eye, a concert of harmonies and harmonic combinations captured, not in the time series, but in the spatial (simultaneously)."[2] Goethe allowed us to see music and architecture differently.

For generations, architecture served as the holder of moments in the history of humanity, historic moments. That is until the book replaced it. As Victor Hugo noted in his book, Notre-Dame de Paris, "This will kill that. The book will kill the edifice." Stories were embedded in architecture.

T3XTURE's previous issues' explorations of texture, pattern, and ornament led us to this archaic word "repose." The late Dr. John Jespersen, whose essay arguing for a modern ornament, appeared in T3XTURE, Issue Number 2, "Ornament is Splendid," emphasized the role of repose in architectural ornament. He cites

1 Halpern, Nathaniel. "Stasis." Episode. Tales from the Loop 1, no. 3. Accessed April 3, 2020. https://www.amazon.com/gp/video/detail/B08BYHJPM7/ref=atv_dp_sharecur.

2 F. W. J. Schelling, Philosophy of Art. Preliminary study, translation and notes by Virginia López-Domínguez. Madrid, Tecnos, 1999, p. 313.

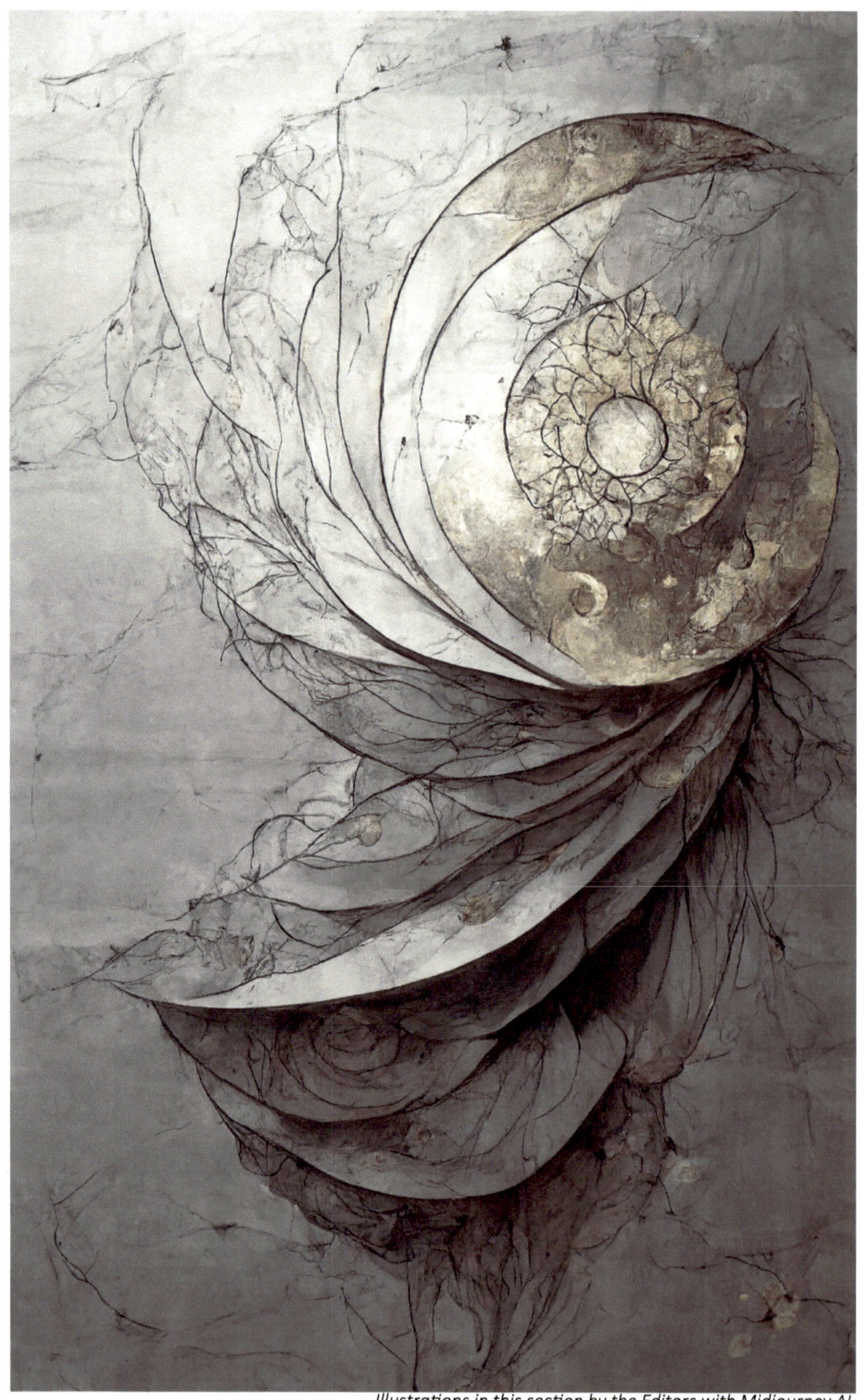

Illustrations in this section by the Editors with Midjourney AI.

Owen Jones' *Propositions Three and Four.* Repose, Jespersen argued was an important aspect of architectural beauty that has been lost in the Modernist insistence on form follows function. For Jespersen, repose was "a pause in the design for contemplation allowed by an interruption in the sequence of spatial events or by some device which detains the eye." In other words, a place for pause and reflection amidst the hustle and bustle of everyday life.

Perhaps there is a way to create an architecture that punctuates our lives with moments of pause and reflection; an architecture that encourages us to slow down and savor the reading experience. A return, of sorts, to a more leisurely pace of life.

Owen Jones *Proposition Three* harkens to the triplet of Vitruvius, *firmitas, utilitas, and venustas*, famously translated into English by Henry Wotton as *firmness, commodity, and delight.* Jones, however, wraps the three into a single word: repose.

"As Architecture, so all works of the Decorative Arts, should possess fitness, proportion, harmony, the result of all which is repose." [3]

Owen Jones' *Proposition Four* then connects repose with a completeness, a fullness: "True beauty results from that repose, which the mind feels when the eye, the intellect, and the affections are satisfied from the absence of any want."[4]

And for Jespersen, repose, is exclusively accessible by the language of ornament:

"Field theory in the Grammar, with its conventionalized ornament based upon nature and the principles of ornamental design throughout history, has a very subtle and civilizing purpose. I would like to point out the two most important propositions in the Grammar: *Propositions Three and Four.* These both deal with repose, which is both an ancient metaphysic and a modern aesthetic. In its fullness, it is a way of life essential for civilization. It means: trust, serenity, tranquility, rest, revitalization, peace and much more that cannot be put into words, much more which is only accessible by the language of ornament."[5]

3 Owen Jones, The Grammar of Ornament (London: Day and Sons, 1856).
4 (Ibid).
5 Jespersen, John Kresten, "Owen Jones' The Grammar of Ornament: Field Theory in the Post-Modern Studio" (1988). Faculty Publications. 440.

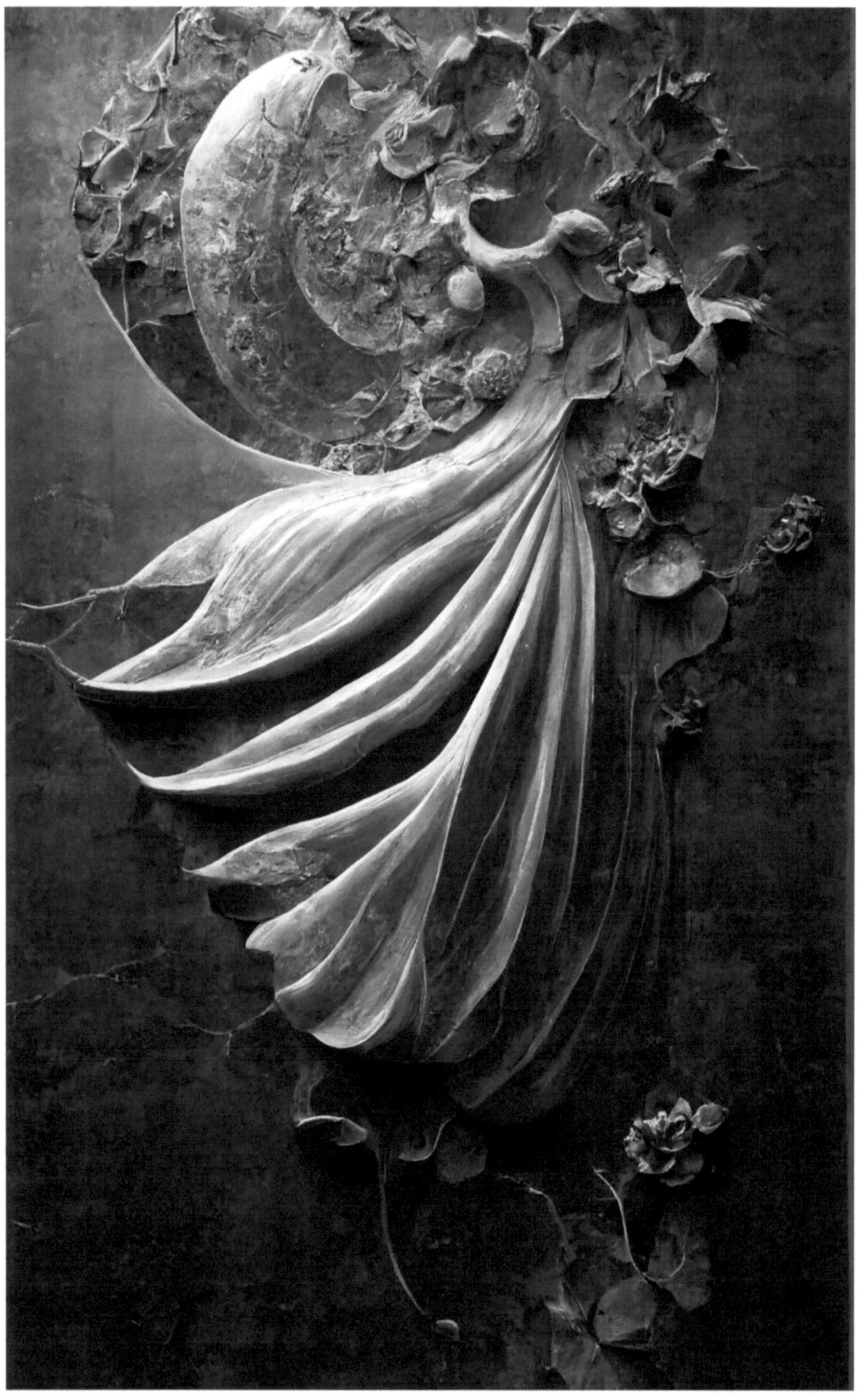

Jespersen continues on to discuss the spiritual aspect of repose:

"Repose is the fundamental aesthetic and metaphysic of ornament, the crown of glory which wisdom bestows on those who believe (Proverbs 4:9)."[6]

Jespersen's claim that repose and ornament are essential for civilization casts a harsh light on the past hundred years of architectural design—a period largely defined by a rejection of ornamentation. The phrases "Ornament is Crime" and "Less is More" dominated architectural discourse in the 20th century, reflecting a shift away from traditional decoration and toward a more streamlined aesthetic. This move away from ornamentation was often justified on the grounds that it would lead to a more efficient and modernist architecture. However, in retrospect, it is clear that this period was characterized not by efficiency or progress, but by a rampant disregard for the environment. It has been a time without repose and an environmentally uncivilized time.

In his essay "In the Cause of Architecture," Frank Lloyd Wright discusses the importance of simplicity and repose in art and architecture. He argues that these qualities are necessary to create a harmonious relationship between the work of art and its surroundings. Fallingwater, one of Wright's most famous buildings, is a clear example of his philosophy in action. The structure is designed to echo the natural forms of the rocks and waterfall around it, creating a sense of balance and harmony. In this way, Fallingwater exemplifies Wright's belief that simplicity and repose are essential to creating a work of art.

To John Ruskin, a meadow or field undisturbed by buildings is the epitome of repose. He criticizes those who would build villas disturbing this repose, saying they do not care about the peace they have disturbed. For Ruskin, repose isn't just physical, but also mental and emotional. Nature has a way of restoring our weary spirits; we should be careful not to destroy this repose with our building and development.[7]

Ruskin's repose is a natural state to be respected:

---

6 (Ibid).

7 Ruskin, John, The Poetry of Architecture. E. T. Cook and Alexander Wedderburn,Editors, London, George Allen, 156, Charing Cross Road, NY, New York: Longmans, Green, and Company 1903.

"...it may be as commonplace as the proprietor likes, provided its proportions be good; but nothing can ever excuse one acute angle, or one decorated pinnacle—both being direct interruption of the repose with which the eye is indulged."[8]

Repose as a sense of protection from danger appears as a state of being for Dante's narrator and his guide, heedless of their personal safety [repose], making their climb in his Divine Comedy:

> "My guide and I did enter, to return
> To the fair world: and heedless of repose
> We climbed, he first, I following his steps,
> Till on our view the beautiful lights of heav'n
> Dawn'd through a circular opening in the cave:
> Thus issuing we again beheld the stars."[9]

Or it might be a state of being as in a repositioning—a pause permitting us to reset, to re-pause or re-position ourselves physically and mentally? Kent Bloomer, a contributor to T3XTURE, Issues #2 and #4, proposes both *re-pause* and *re-positioning*. "The 'pause' proposes a re-pausing... a stopping before z . But also provides a time for reflection—relating to TIME, and the term "position" is more about the spatial arrangement. Re-positioning (re-arranging) is less about returning—relating to SPACE....both conditions propose discussions regarding repose qua ornamentation." [10] However, his thoughts may apply equally to a period of pandemic and a century-long period of rejecting ornament.

Edward S. Casey, contributor to T3XTURE Issue #4, cites Bachelard's books, The Poetics of Reverie and The Poetics of Space. He proposes repose as a state of mind.

Pausing is *a caesura*, a stasis in the flow, a moment of repose in which we can think through the predicament we have put ourselves into and from which we must extricate ourselves by putting the escalation of our lives into pause mode. It's a matter of finding the right re-pose, pausing again and again and.."[11]

---

8 (Ibid)

9 Alighieri, Dante. 2009. The Divine Comedy. Translated by H. F. Cary. Wordsworth Classics of World Literature. Ware, England: Wordsworth Editions.

10 Correspondence between the editors and Mr. Bloomer.

11 Correspondence between the editors and Mr. Casey.

Bachelard takes repose to another state—a state of being in the world and in the world of our dreams.. He finds repose in private daydreams and in dark places, corners, caves, and nests.

"The soul does not live on the edge of time. It finds its rest in the universe imagined by reverie..."[12]

"Cosmic images are possessions of the solitary soul which is the principle of all solitude."[13]

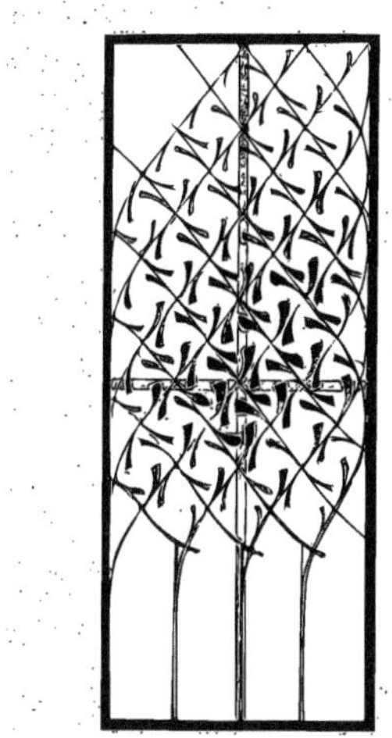

Diagram of W. Springfield Library Window/ Kent Bloomer Studio

And then we must consider the opposite of repose: motion (energy). Combined, repose and motion (energy) form a diad essential to art. For Claude Bragdon, the eye and the ear draw to the opposing extremes of stasis and change.

"The eye longs for repose in some serene radiance or stately sequence, while the ear delights in contrast and continual change."[14]

Poet, critic, educator, and founder of Aesthetic Realism, Eli Siegal asked: "Is there in painting an effect which arises from the being together of Repose and Energy in the artist's mind?—can both repose and energy be seen in a painting's line and color, plane and volume, surface and depth, detail and composition?—and is the true effect of a good painting on the spectator one that makes at once for repose and intensity, serenity and stir?"[15]

In this issue we explore this diad of repose and motion via an interview, several original essays, and real and speculative projects.

---

12 Bachelard, Gaston 2010. The Poetics of Space. Harrison, NY: Beacon Press.
13 (Ibid).
14 Claude Bragdon & the Beautiful Necessity: Eleven Essays. 2010. RIT Cary Graphic Arts Press.
15 Eli Siegel, "Is Beauty the Making One of Opposites?" Journal of Aesthetics & Art Criticism, December 1955; Ante, 1964.

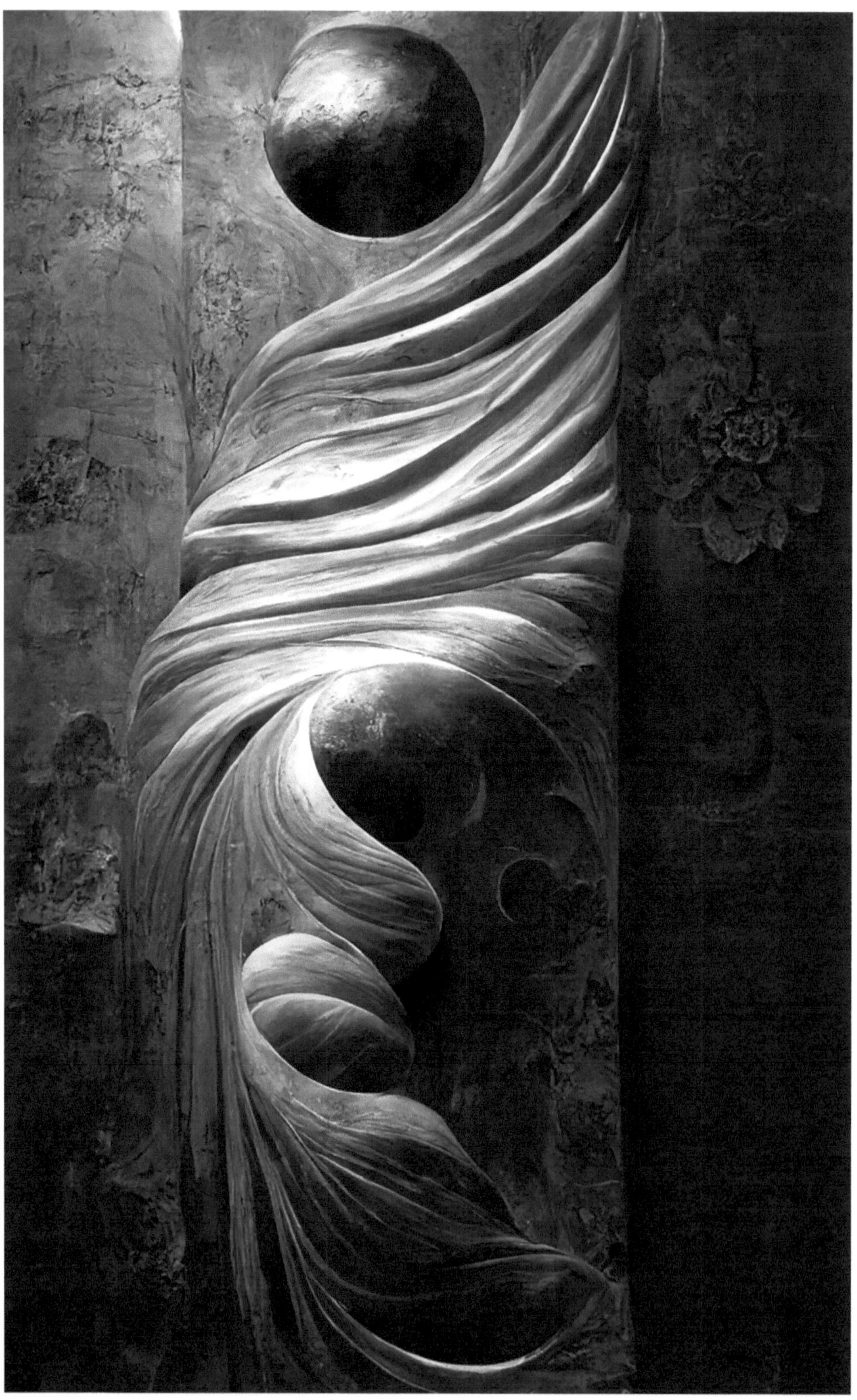

"Capturing a Moment," our interview with novelist, essayist, physicist, and educator, Alan Paige Lightman, covers a broad range of topics in his career and touches on the experiential aspects of repose. To Lightman, renowned physicist and author of Einstein's Dream" and more recently, Searching for Stars on an Island in Maine, and more, repose is a state of mind.

In "The Ornamentor Within" Ioana Barac discusses how to create an ecosystem of meaningful experiences in an existing lobby space.

"Terra Turrita Felix," a project by architect, Beniamino Servino architectural practice based in Caserta, Italy, is the focus of our essay on his geological repose to volcanoes, "Vesuvius in Repose."

"Rising Unity" describes a Traveling Memorial Sculpture for Victims of Opioid Overdose. It was commissioned by Demand Zero & For Cameron and realized by Atelier Cue in 2020.

Nicole Cullinan, who writes on architecture and the arts in Melbourne, Australia asks, "Has Our Love Affair with Open-Plan Living Finally Ended?" After extended lockdowns in Melbourne and with many in the world working from home, is the open-plan becoming obsolete? The lingering question is: can one find repose in a house with no corners?

Miriam Gusevich, of GM2 Architects reflects on the value of repose in times of crisis in a piece titled "Urban Pentimento: stories of repose, repentance, and repair. "

"Plug-In Bridge: From Hermes to Hestia." A project by Vincent Peu Duvallon, DESA Architect, RIBA, Assoc. AIA, Wenzhou, Zhejiang, China, transforms an infrastructure into a series of public and resting spaces in their proposal for the valley of Caocun, in the south of China.

In "A Place for Peace: Taming an Urban Mèlange," architect Khashayar Shahkolahy brings a tranquil respite to the hustle and bustle of city life. His proposal for a nondenominational sanctuary offers harried students refuge in a chaotic urban intersection; instead of disrupting nature on an existing campus lawn, he proposes a calming oasis amidst the chaos.

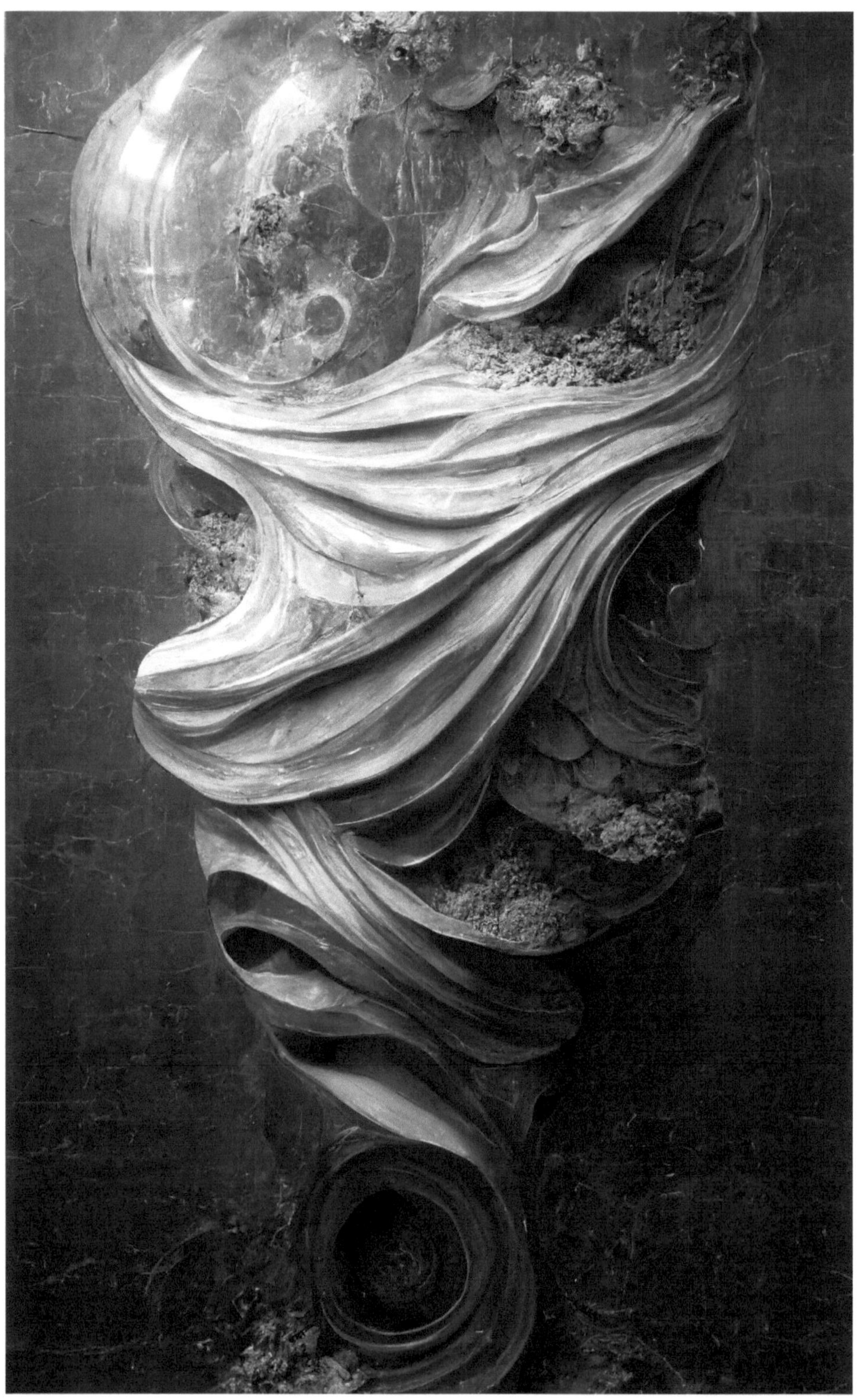

In response to this issue's topic, Craig Purcell diagrams a framework for repose and motion in the flat plane of a painting in process. Guidelines forming the framework that carries repose move through time and space.

For Antoine Predock, the body in motion—choreographed in the landscape—is a theme throughout his body of work.

Janet Little Jeffers photographs, appearing in the interview with Alan Lightman, are part of her ongoing body of work that emerged from many hours of hiking in the woods during the months of the COVID-19 pandemic. She says:

My photographic practice usually involves outdoor exploration, but limited to areas close to home, I found myself walking the same trails in a meditative practice. Not only was I seeking peace in a time of anxiety, but I was also looking deeply into the familiar terrain to discover something new.

Drawn repeatedly to streams and marshy areas, I observed that in areas of still water, the surface often contains iridescent colors and metallic textures, the product not of petroleum, but of beneficial iron-oxidizing bacteria naturally produced in groundwater-fed streams. The colorful surfaces, combined with elements of fallen leaves and other organic matter, distorted reflections of trees and sky, and the murky shapes of rocks and stream bed beneath the surface, all transform the water we take for granted into a source of mystery awaiting discovery.

Where Lightman pondered the motion of the cosmos from his boat in Maine, Jeffers finds it in the reflections at her feet.

Special thanks to Edward S. Casey for his support and encouragement.

Illustrations in this section created by the Editors using Midjourney AI.
The prompts included, "cosmos, repose, architectural ornament, and patina."
The illustration on the following page was also generated with Midjourney AI using the prompt: "searching for the stars on a lake in Maine."

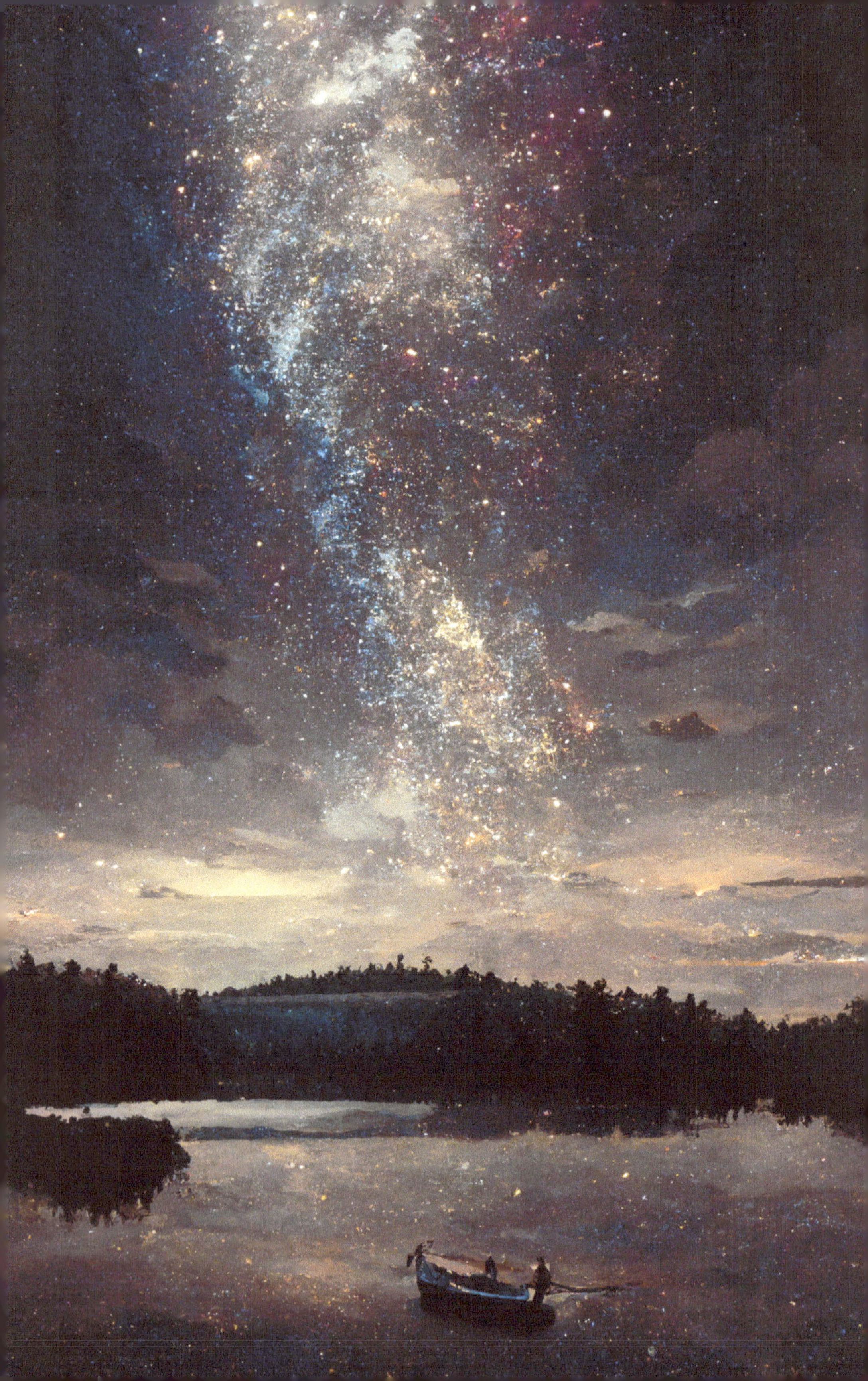

IN THIS ISSUE

“Repose is the quiet of our inner self. My inner self is that part of me that imagines, that dreams, that explores, that is constantly questioning who I am and what is important to me.”

Alan Lightman

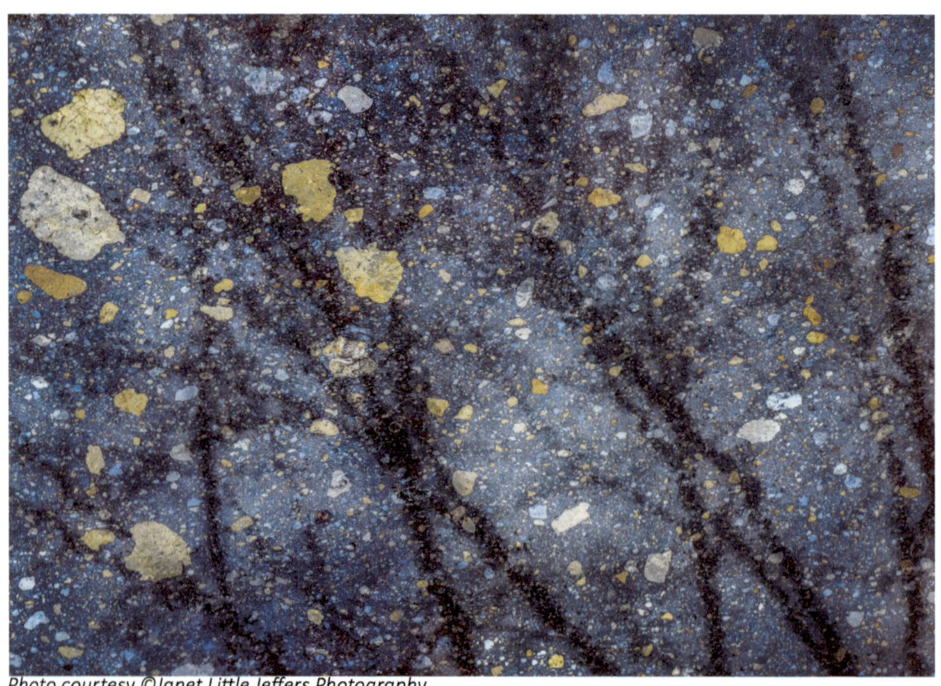

Photo courtesy ©Janet Little Jeffers Photography

CAPTURING A MOMENT

Best known for his book, Einstein's Dreams, Alan Paige Lightman is a writer, physicist, and social entrepreneur. At MIT, he held a joint faculty position in both the sciences and the humanities. In addition to many essays and scientific publications, his fiction and poetry include:

> Einstein's Dreams (1993), Good Benito (1995), The Diagnosis (2000), Reunion (2003), Ghost (2007), Song of Two Worlds (poetry) (2009), Mr g (2012), and Three Flames (2019)[27]

In 2001, he established MIT's "Communication Requirement," which requires all undergraduates to have training in writing and speaking each of their four years. His extensive writing and thinking span the sciences and the humanities.

We asked him about topics in several of his recent books—books we highly recommend. His most recent book, Probable Impossibilities, was published in 2021, and his 2018 book, Searching for Stars on an Island in Maine, will become a movie.

T3X: *Science and architecture writing is often obtuse and unnecessarily challenging. The Sokal Hoax Papers brought this to light in the mid-1990s. Some architectural publications also seem to be unduly complex. More recently though, architectural publications are more like marketing material than actual criticism or analysis. In 2001 you instituted the Communication Requirement at MIT. Can you tell us a bit about the intent and outcomes of the program?*

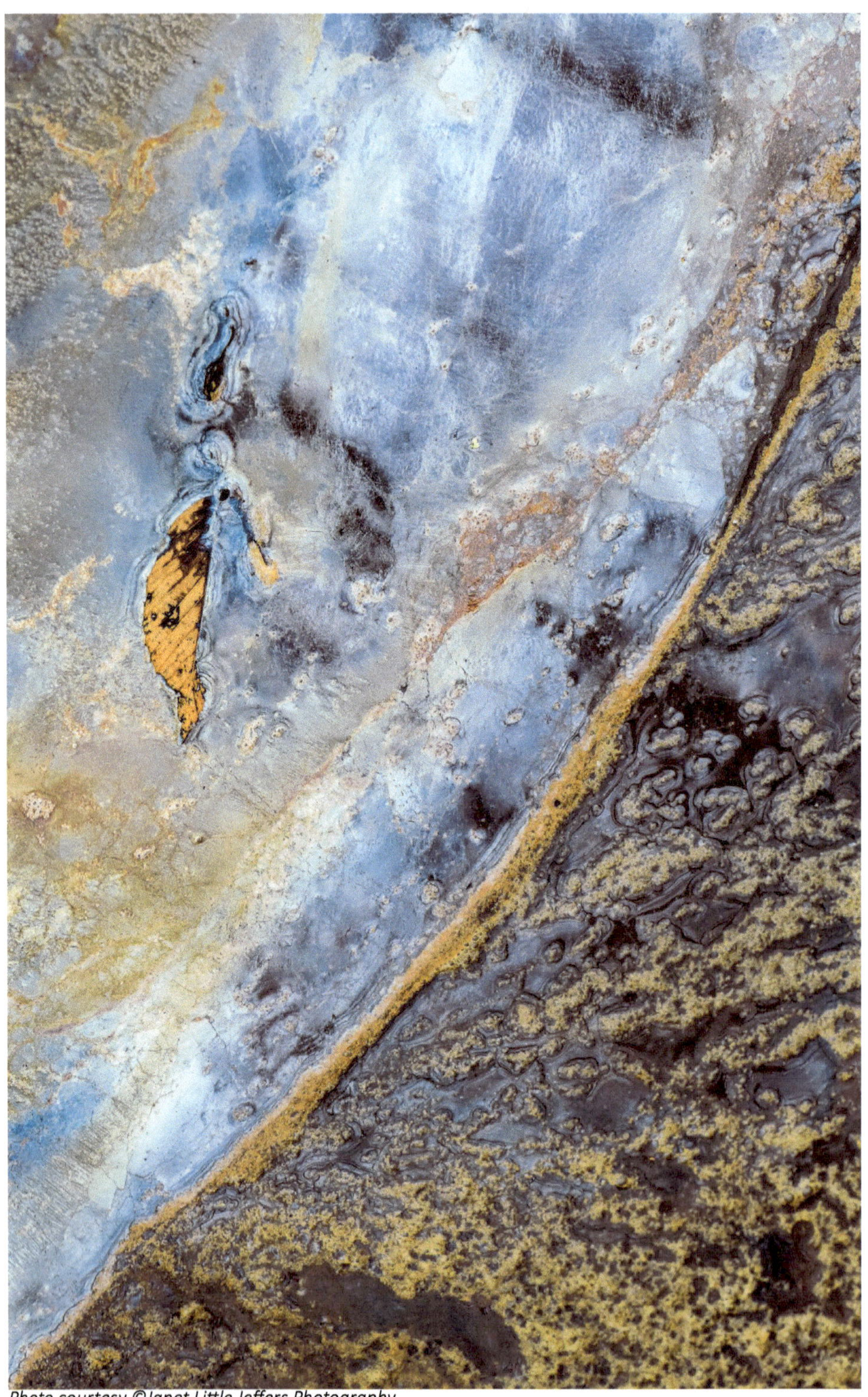

Photo courtesy ©Janet Little Jeffers Photography

APL: In most liberal arts universities, students automatically do a lot of writing in all four years of their university education. Such writing goes hand in hand with developing their critical ability and also ability to express themselves clearly and forcefully. At many science and technology oriented universities, that writing and communication practice does not happen nearly as much – and that was the case at MIT until we instituted the Communication Requirement two decades ago. We live in an age of science and technology, which is becoming increasingly interdisciplinary. It is more and more important for scientists and engineers to be able to communicate with a wide spectrum of other people in the humanities, social sciences, and policy making. So, it is crucial for scientists and engineers to have those communication skills. Our Communication Requirement requires each student to take at least one course each year that includes an intensive writing or speaking component. After twenty years, our graduates have been better prepared to function in the world today. They are better speakers and better writers, and their job opportunities are increased.

T3X: *Italian Renaissance gardens, such as the Villa di Castello in Florence, were geometrical configurations of carefully manicured plantings and walks. They were human-controlled Nature, a safe, liminal space between the human-made city and the dangerous wilderness beyond. In that era, Nature (wilderness) was considered a hostile environment occupied by all sorts of hazards and ruffians. In today's discourse, Nature, the earth, is seen as fragile and to be protected. In "Our Lonely Home in Nature," in your most recent book, Probable Impossibilities, you describe the power of Nature. Contrary to conventional wisdom, you affirm that Nature will survive; it does not have our well-being in mind. We must protect ourselves. How might we reshape the conversation about the 'fragility of Nature? Should we?*

APL: I would argue that it is we human beings, and the ecosystem required for our survival, that is fragile, not Nature. From a cosmic perspective, Nature takes on many forms: black holes, planets whose atmosphere is pure sulfuric acid, jets of subatomic particles powered by magnetic fields, radio waves, neutron stars in which the mass of a star is packed into a region only 1 mile across. Nature is not fragile. It exists in an enormous range of temperature and density, material composition, and environments of many kinds. On the other hand, we human beings require a narrow range of temperature, atmosphere, and available resources. In protecting that environment, we are protecting ourselves. The action of protecting our environment can be framed as protecting Nature, and the steps taken for that protection are the same whether described in terms of our

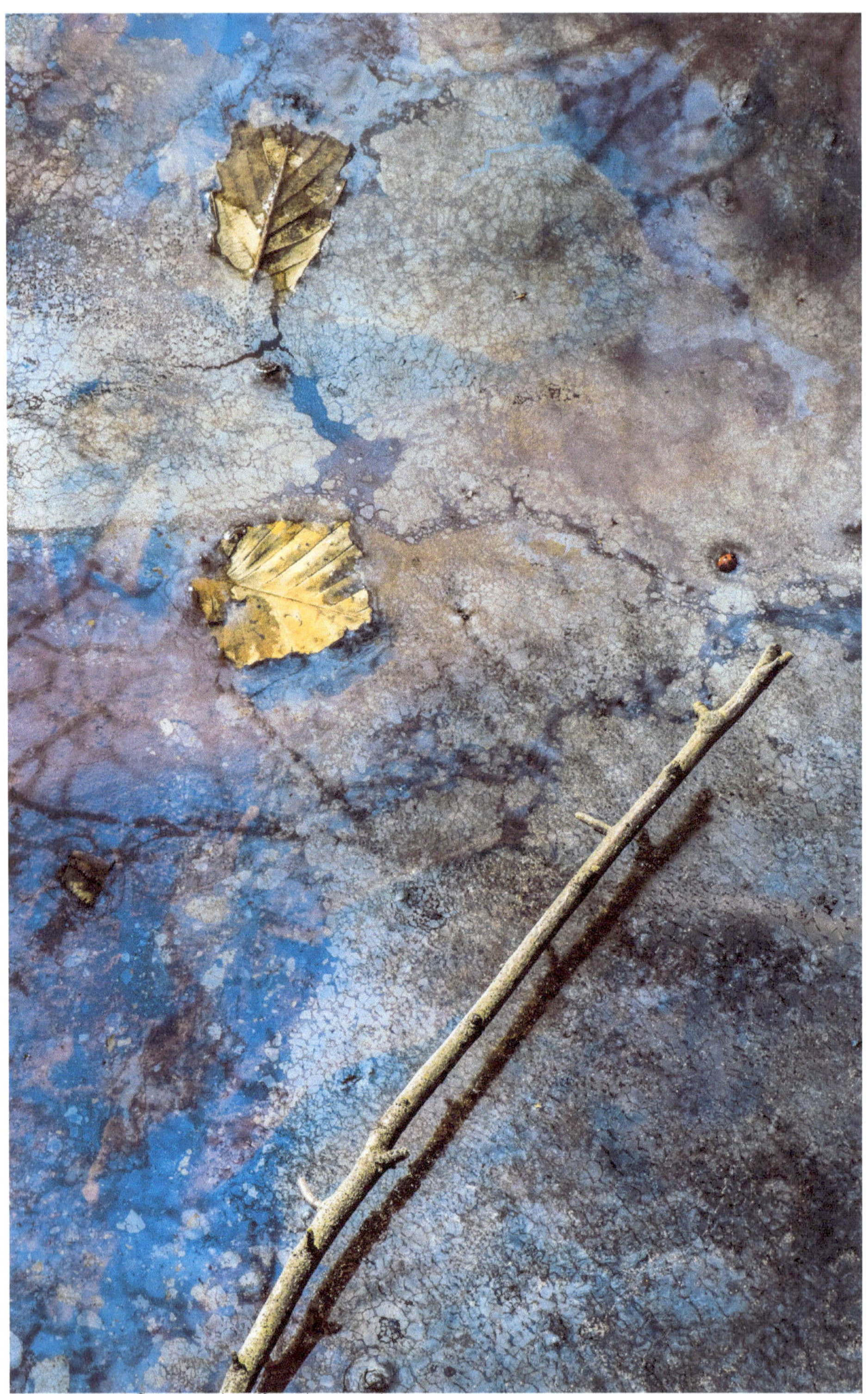

Photo courtesy ©Janet Little Jeffers Photography

own needs or those of Nature. But, in reality, Nature needs no protection. It is we human beings that need protection.

T3X: *As we elaborated in the narrative above, humans have embued their physical environments with tropes or symbols connecting to nature and the cosmos with ornament for thousands of years. We are now at least three generations removed from a collective understanding of the role of ornament, i.e., linking our environments to nature. In preparing for this issue on Motion and Repose, we thought of the chapter "Motion," in your book, Searching for Stars on an Island in Maine. You discuss the profound experience you had lying on your back, looking at the stars. You felt drawn into the cosmos and yet felt the stillness. We might call that stillness "repose." Since most of the world lives in urban areas with artificial light, we lack an awareness of the motion of the cosmos that, say, a sailor who navigates by the stars has. Or a shepherd in the desert. How might we, as architects, physicists, and writers, renew that cosmic experience?*

APL: A big part of our lack of sufficient "repose" and connection to nature in today's world is our obsession with speed, information, and the internet. The pace of life has always been driven by the speed of communication, which has increased exponentially in recent years with the internet and the smart phones. Many of us feel that we must be plugged into the grid twenty-four hours a day. We take our smart phones with us when we walk in the woods or when we dine at restaurants. So, first of all, we need to slow down. As the Buddhists say, we need to be mindful of the present moment. When we witness the mist rising from a pond in early morning, we should simply experience the scene, rather than rush to record it with our phones and post it on Instagram. Second, on a regular basis we should make an effort to escape from the "built environment." Most of us, even those who live in cities, can find open fields, forests, lakes somewhere nearby. Spending time in these places replenishes the spirit.

T3X: *We so often see opposites as being fundamental to life and art. Your books document our understanding of the cosmos as changing from a fixed position (universe in repose) to an ever-expanding system (universe in motion). What is the role of repose in a cosmos always on the move?*

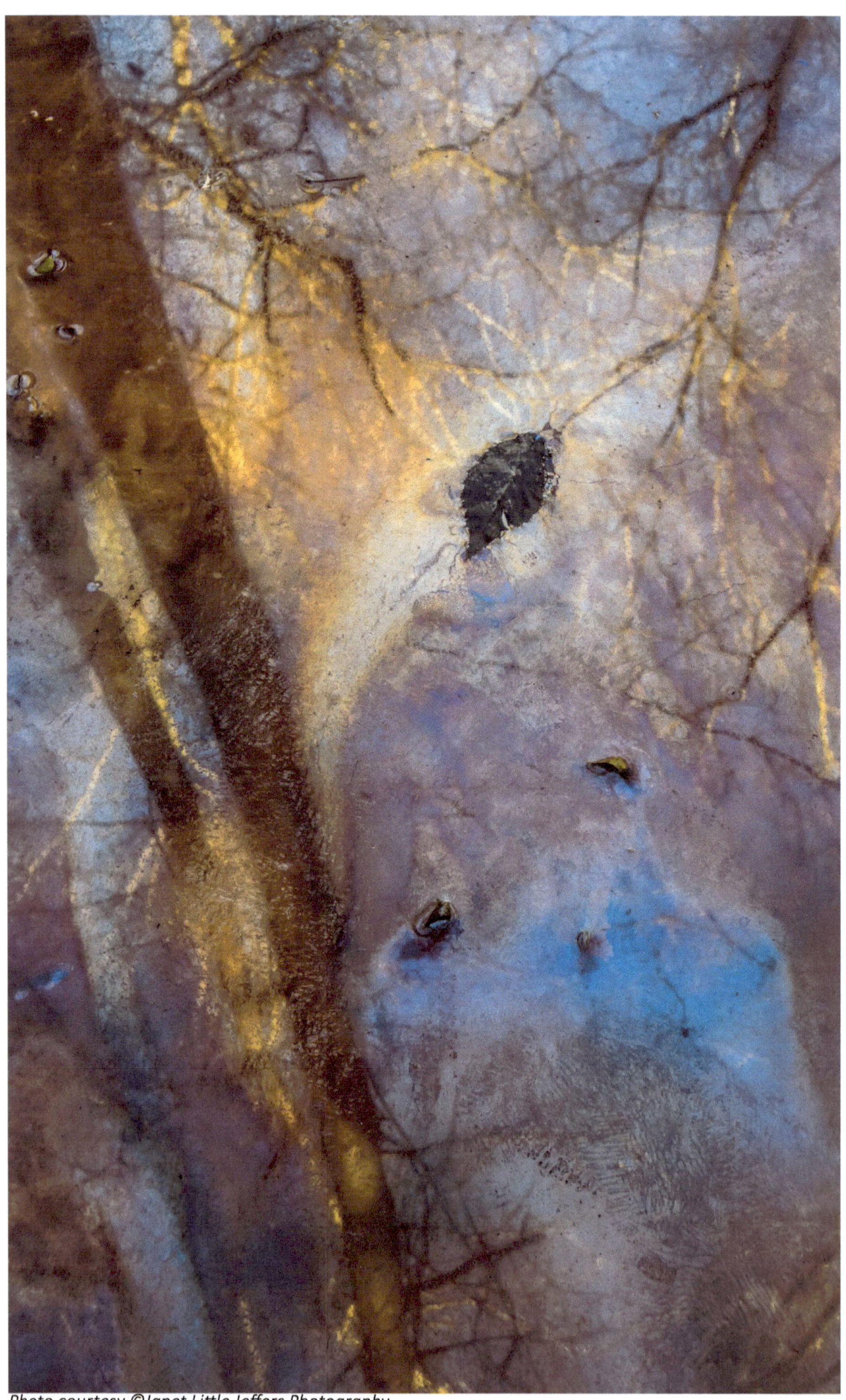

Photo courtesy ©Janet Little Jeffers Photography

APL: Repose is a state of mind, not a condition of the outside world. Repose is the quiet of our inner self. My inner self is that part of me that imagines, that dreams, that explores, that is constantly questioning who I am and what is important to me. My inner self is my true freedom. My inner self roots me to me, and to the ground beneath me. The sunlight and soil that nourishes my inner self are solitude and personal reflection. When I listen to my inner self, I hear the breathing of my spirit. Those breaths are so tiny and delicate, I need stillness to hear them, I need slowness to hear them. I need vast, silent spaces in my mind. I need privacy. Without the breathing and the voice of my inner self, I am a prisoner of the world around me.

T3X: *It seems that you and Kent Bloomer, who we interviewed in Issue #2, have invested your careers in finding our place in the cosmos; but have come at it from different perspectives. Through his understanding of architecture as not only a background for the drama of human activities, Kent has seen the renewal of ornament as a lens through which we appreciate nature and cosmos. He has created a modern model of ornament that reframes our understanding of our place in the world. In your essay, "Nothing But the Truth," in Dance for Two, you write of your experience seeing the cave paintings in Font-de-Gaume. Pure science, like art and music, deals with truth. What do you think might be the pure truth our civilization leaves behind?*

APL: The truths in science are more objective and durable than the truths in art, since there is always an external reality against which to test scientific truths – the behavior of the natural world – and that reality is constant in time, not subject to changes in culture and fashion. Galileo's quantitative law for falling bodies can never go out of style, whereas Cubism and Beethoven's Moonlight Sonata will wax and wane with the centuries, perhaps one day disappearing altogether. Our civilization will definitely leave behind the discovered truths of relativity, quantum physics, the composition and structure of DNA, etc. In the world of the humanities and ethics, I believe that the Golden Rule: "Do unto others as you would have them to unto you" will never go out of style. In all the different truths claimed by various religions, I believe the Golden Rule can be found in all of them and will have enduring acceptance.

Photo on following spread courtesy ©Janet Little Jeffers Photography

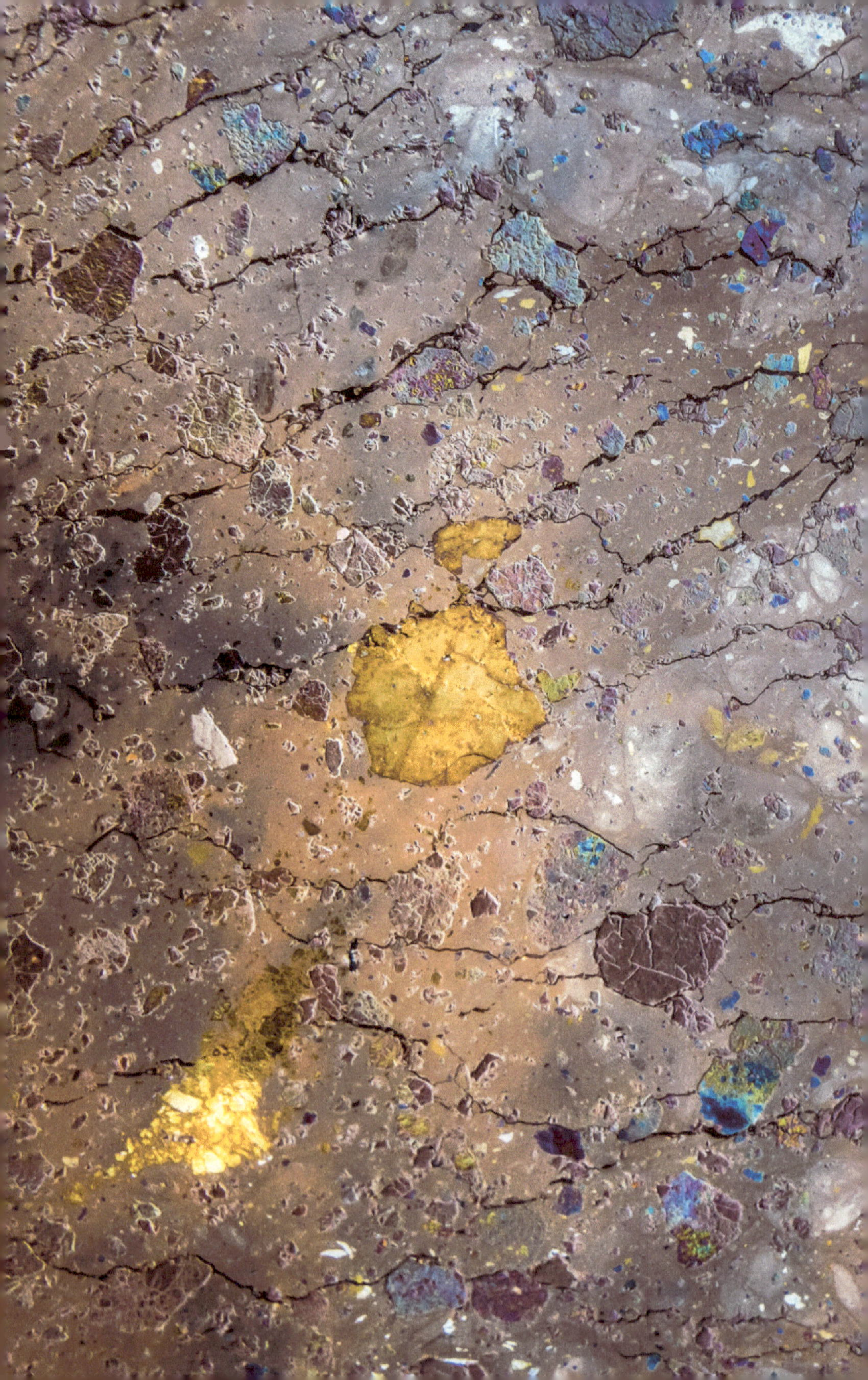

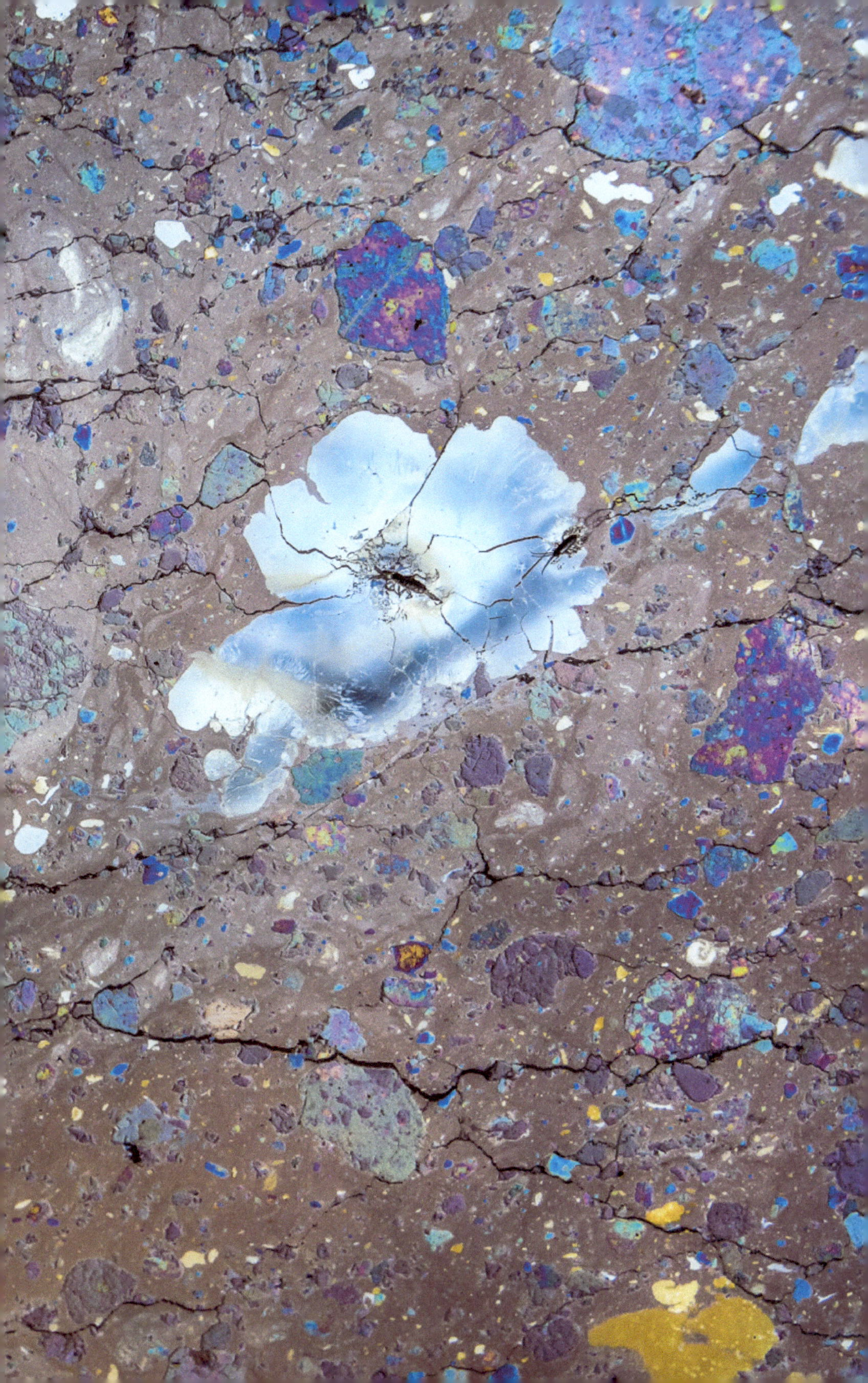

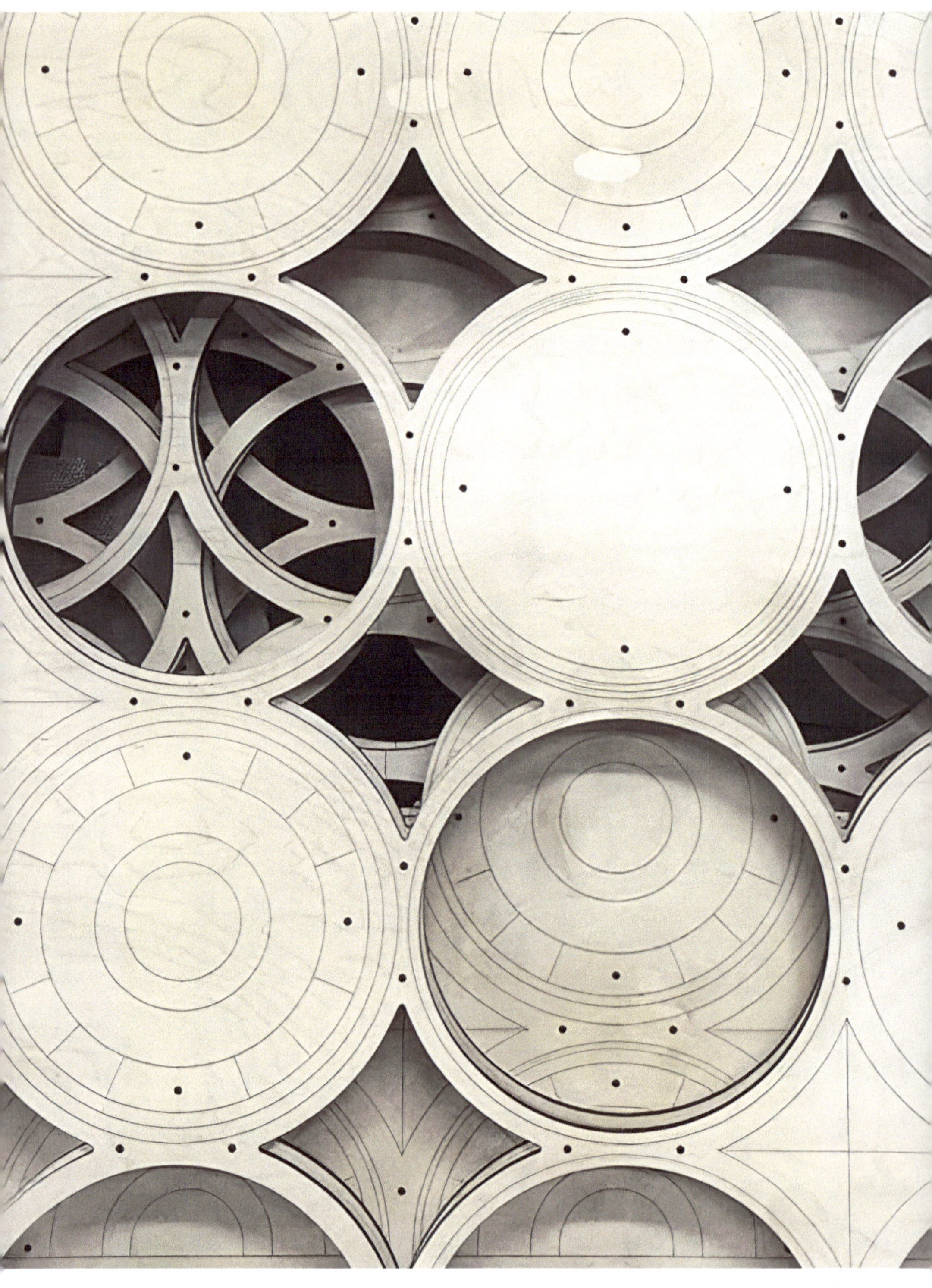

Figure 6

IOANA BARAC

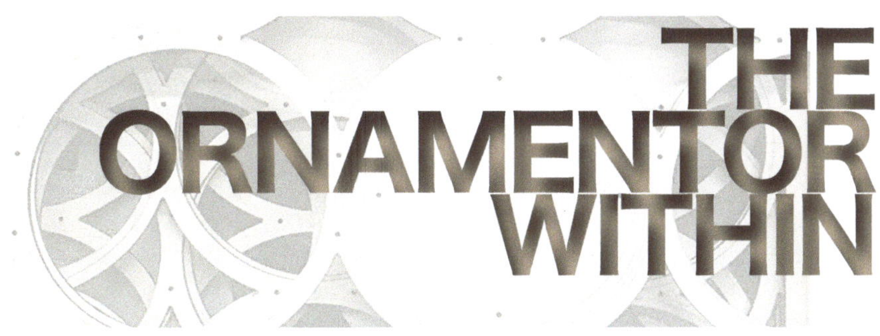

THE ORNAMENTOR WITHIN

Notes on Energy and Repose Along the Making of (a piece of) Ornament

Beyond "Less is more" and "Less is a bore," our place-making seeks those special moments where more can be, in effect, more. Placemaking is, in our practice, the act of strategically intervening in a neutral space[1] to create an ecosystem of identifiable, meaningful experiences, turning space into place: place = space + meaning. Placemaking turns space into place, where place = space + meaning. As makers of architecture and art, we concern ourselves with the physically built container and the objects present in it *and* with the inter-action with these as unique, specific experiences in time and space, anchored in form and content in a particular locality.

We propose that what gives meaning to an experience is, first and foremost, the willingness to participate in it.[2] That meaning is not an inherent, objective quality of the object or place but is conditioned by one's willingness to engage with them and is actualized in the engagement itself. Framing this inter-action in terms of energy and repose, we see the creation of meaning as a transformation in one's mind-body state. Each individual comes in contact with our work with an a priori internal energetic state which can be modified by the encounter. Our aspiration is to enhance this energy such that the experience be carried on, beyond the encounter, in action and memory. Embracing the aesthetic and haptic experience as activators, we delegate the creation of meaning to sensory, psychological, and mental arousal and engagement.

1 *"Neutral" in this context means to absence of remarkable features – in that it does not prompt noticing, interacting, lingering.*

2 *Exploring the "mind's eye" in his book "Hallucinations", Oliver Sachs notes that 'visions' can be perceived as meaningless when not relatable with the observer's circumstances (Sachs 2013, 229).*

The more an event invites interest and focus on it, the more engaging it is. The arousal we seek is less through quantity of stimulation and more through its qualities and nature: these must fit and resonate with our sense of inner and outer reality.[3]

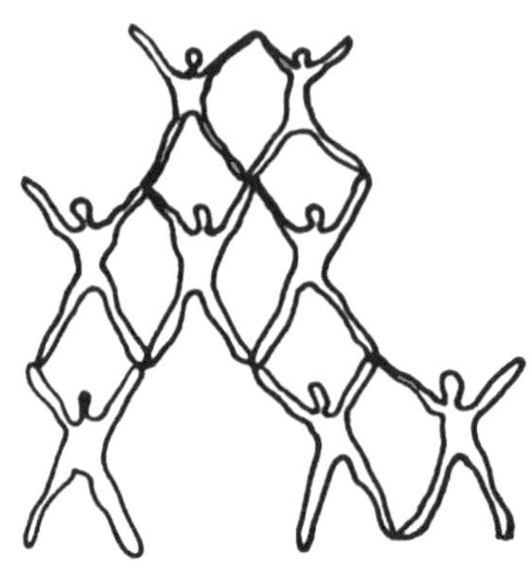

Figure 1

The more resonance and alignment, the more intense and multi-faceted the inter-action: In such a fortunate state, we propose, the event fully experienced becomes a meaningful and memorable encounter.[4] Place becomes the locality of an experience worth having and, at the same time, the locality worth experiencing.

Place is a charge, charging reality, reverberating through sensations and perceptions in imagination and memory.[5] Place-making, through this lens, is an orchestration of charged and charging events of varying intensities. Instances of "less" (absence, scarcity, uniformity) and "more" (presence, abundance, elaboration) are organized to create a perception of composed balance within the environment and dynamic equilibrium between body-mind and environment as one moves or lingers within. In a reverse symmetry, occasions of "less" invite passage while those of "more" invite pause. Overall and individually, these instances of repose span a range of states of balance, enacted at different scales and speeds of travel and encounter. Acknowledging a continuity – or a mirroring – between physical and psychological realities, these tensions are bound to reverberate in enhanced subjective experience.[6]

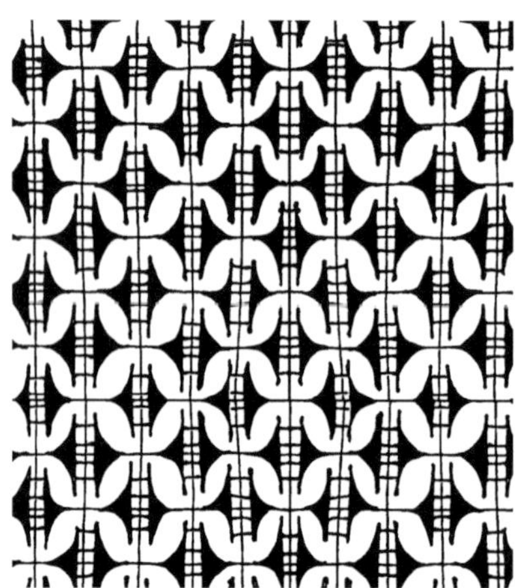

Figure 2

---

3 *Exploring the "mind's eye" in his book "Hallucinations", Oliver Sachs notes that 'visions' can be perceived as meaningless when not relatable with the observer's circumstances (Sachs 2013, 229). Sensed or imagined, their perception changes in heightened states of arousals or in formalized cultural practices, or when recognized as mirrors of each other (ibid., 132).*

4 *Not necessarily related but, we believe, both contributing to the sense of place and meaning. This resonance and fulfillment felt on multiple levels points to Owen Jones' notion of repose as that "which the mind feels when the eye, the intellect, and the affections, are satisfied from the absence of any want" (Jespersen, 2008, 152).*

5 *"Sensation and perception are two separate processes that are very closely related. Sensation is input about the physical world obtained by our sensory receptors, and perception is the process by which the brain selects, organizes, and interprets these sensations. In other words, senses are the physiological basis of perception. Perception of the same senses may vary from one person to another because each person's brain interprets stimuli differently based on that individual's learning, memory, emotions, and expectations." ("Sensation and Perception", accessed November 11, 2020).*

6 *As Pepperell writes, "the energetic patterns arriving at the visual receptors have their counterparts as 'field processes' in the nervous system" (Pepperell 2018, 426).*

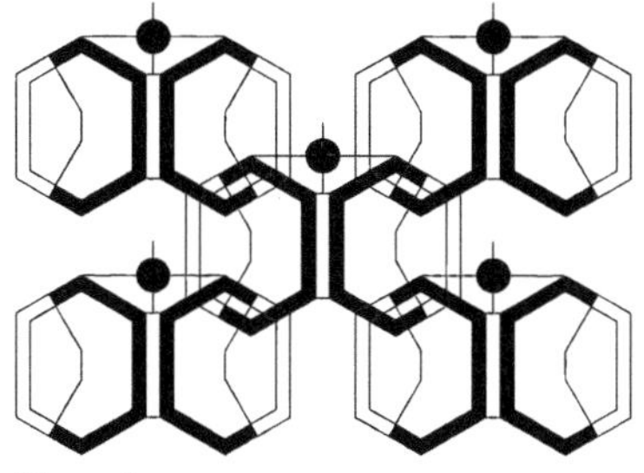
Figure 3

From serene contemplation to embodied tension, place-making entails a choreography of changing energies, alternating depths, and heights of experience.[7]

Among the many decorative interventions at our disposal, ornament is, by its nature, a reliable carrier of visual energy, with the potential to occasion the full spectrum of states of repose in contrast or harmony with its surroundings.[8]

Because of what it is and how it functions, or, better said, because of how and why we've been making and using it across continents and eras, we propose ornament is particularly suited for effecting an intensified experience of place.

We see ornamenting as born from our ability to read the patterns of the cosmos internal and external to our minds and from the impulse to translate these patterns at the human scale. From our need to make sense of them, to reveal them, and to relish in their mystery and beauty;[9] to inscribe this understanding on bodies, objects, and surfaces, claiming ownership over them and imparting, through them, energy and meaning.

Sharing visual form with mental imagery in rituals of drug-induced altered states of consciousness, or in mind-events such as migraine auras, as stimulus or result of cognitive structures,[10] patterns can provide (or, for some, recall) pleasure and transcendence on demand. "There seems to have been, throughout human history, a need to externalize and make art from these internal experiences, from the cross-hatchings of prehistoric cave paintings to the swirling psychedelic art of the 1960s. Do the arabesques and hexagons in our minds, built into our brain's organization, provide us with our first intimations of

---

7 *To use a sailing metaphor: while sailing, water, ship, sailor, and wind are in a state of dynamic equilibrium, of energy exchange, of sustained movement and tension. Such balance can be achieved on smooth or rough waters, with even or gusty winds. For as long as the balance is maintained, the system is in equilibrium, but this equilibrium can have a range of qualities. The kinetic and potential energies at play – the peaks and valleys of the waves and of the winds, the transfers in the corresponding action and reaction, the contraction of the muscles responding to these changes – result in vastly different qualities of balance.*

8 *"The contrast to the decorated (A) state is its non-decorated ("PLAIN") opposite (non-A) – in line with the A-non-A perspective on meaning." This tensioned juxtaposition escalates the affective tension (Valsiner 2008, 70). Moreover, the decorated state or, more accurately, the ornamented state (in keep with Bloomer & Jespersen's clarification of the terms (Bloomer & Jespersen 2015), which is our reading of what Valsiner means in this context), itself presents varied levels of visual tension, through subdued or alert designs.*

9 *Where the artist strives to creates mysteries and the scientist is generally inclined to solve them (Pepperell 2018, 419), the ornamentor is comfortable with both revealing and concealing (in content and in placement). Because of this, ornament may be most suitable as common ground for art and science, and the interdisciplinary explorations of energy and the brain, aesthetic experience and consciousness discussed by Pepperell.*

10 *"In Mechanisms of Hallucinations, ... Kluver spoke of the tendency to "geometrization" in the brain's visual system, and he regarded all such geometrical hallucinations as permutations of four fundamental "form constants" (de identified these as lattices, spirals, cobwebs, and tunnels). He implied that such constants must reflect something about the organization, the functional architecture, of the visual cortex..." (Sachs 2013, 98). See follow-up research and development of models (Stokes 2013).*

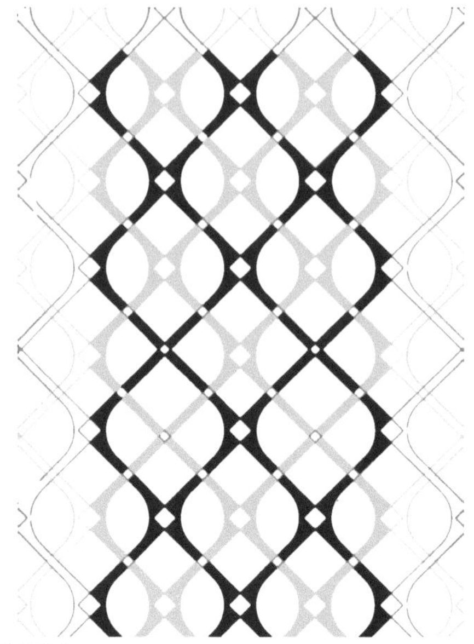
Figure 4

formal beauty?" "There is an increasing feeling among neuro-scientists that self-organizing activity in vast populations of visual neurons is a prerequisite of visual perception – that that is how seeing begins. Spontaneous self-organization is not restricted to living systems; one may see it in the formation of snow crystals, in the roiling and eddies of turbulent water, in specific oscillating chemical reactions. Also, self-organization may produce geometries and patterns in space and time," which "allow us to experience not only a universal of neural functioning but a universal of nature itself." (Sachs 2013, 132). Be it because, in excited states, the structure of the visual cortex generates default patterns, inspiring us to recreate them, or because the patterns capture essential realities of our textured world, ornament may embody pleasure and transcendence.[11] While other actions (meditation, religious practices, art) can satisfy these needs, patterns encountered in the world outside, like those inside, may offer a particular form of and shortcut to their satisfaction.[12]

Ornament is a visual language with its vocabulary of forms charged with literal or symbolic meaning, a language of signs "which come from the deeper regions of human nature where mimicry, gesture, song, and dance originate" (Smeets, Rene, quoted in Jespersen, 2008, 150).[13] Ornament reveals rhythms and movement. Its tropes share characteristics of organization and form across cultures: repetitions, interlockings, variations of lines, geometric shapes, abstracted plant, animal and human figures. Their formal relationships transpose the natural laws and phenomena in figures "serving as energy-diagrams rather than symbols", entangled in rigid geometries, express "the convergence of dynamic and rigid forces in nature" and visualize "the power and shape of differentiation itself." Displayed in metered relationships, like words in verses, like beats in drum calls, ornament reveals rhythms and movement and connects our material reality with the cosmos, "visualizing the order and harmony of the universe" (Bloomer 2019, 22, 25).

11 *"To live on a day-to-day basis is insufficient for human beings; we need to transcend...; we need meaning, understanding...; we need to see overall patterns in our lives." (Sachs 2013, 90)*

12 *"To live on a day-to-day basis is insufficient for human beings; we need to transcend...; we need meaning, understanding...; we need to see overall patterns in our lives." (Sachs 2013, 90) "[...] at a humbler level, drugs" [and possibly ornaments, as sensorial enhancers] "are used not so much to illuminate or expand or concentrate the mind, to "cleanse the doors of perception", but for the sense of pleasure and euphoria they create." (Sachs 2013, 92)*

13 *Note that all these built-in impulses or practices of communication and expression are movements!*

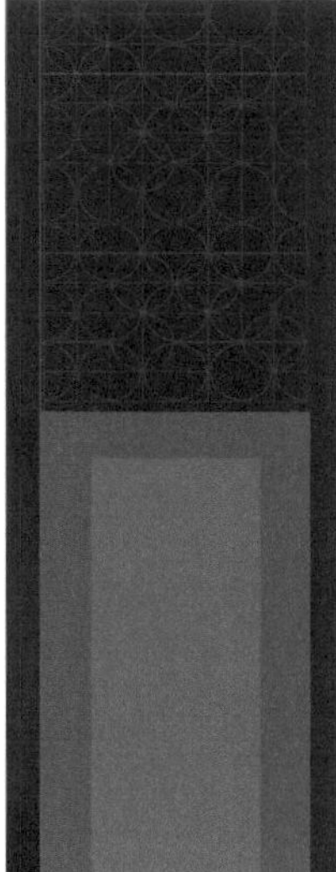

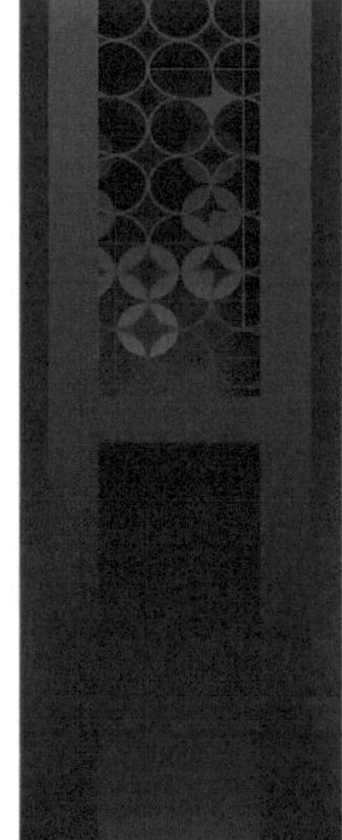

Figure 5

Cycles and rhythms connect us, enacting the fundamental longings of the psyche for continuity in space and time. "Genealogical patterns," such as the tracings on earth of bodies touching limbs (Fig. 1), or weavings of abstracted figures (Fig. 2), further abstracted in expansive networks of lines (Fig. 3), join one to many in "patterns of continuity." Impressively similar in various iterations, such patterns interlock individuals within and across generations in social and cosmic families. (Fig, 4) (Schuster & Carpenter 1996, 81, 94) Anchored in material objects, these actualize continuity beyond here and now, transcending space and time, body and death.

Ornament marks threshold and is threshold. It bridges and intertwines the material and the spiritual, the rational and the irrational, the abstract and the figural, embracing and embodying contradiction and coherence, subjective and objective reality, body and mind. As such, it thrives "in transitional places able to address two or more worlds simultaneously. [...] Such places are edge worlds in which the energy of ornament's motions can unite with the gravity of its holders" and, joining material with "the timeless order of cosmos" expand our living space." (Bloomer 2019, 25)

Ornament and patterns are present in formalized practices and environments, in objects and spaces of ritual, the edges where the sacred and the profane converge. When merging its energies and transcendent qualities with the mass of the physical object, ornament morphs into the form and function of its holder and, in turn, transforms it, making the ordinary extraordinary. The super-added element is a literal and conceptual form of charge: the object, dressed in ceremonial attire, is asked to carry on its enhanced mission.

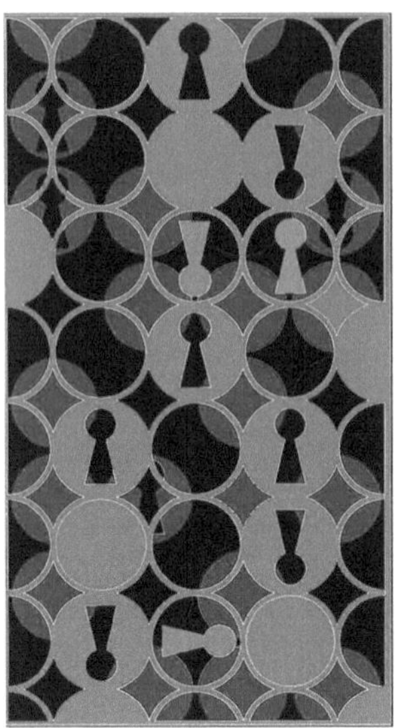
Figure 6

The Making of "Keys"

In the Canopy Lobby,[14] North Bethesda, concentrated visual energy guides the movement through the environment, directing the sensory and the affective changes associated with experiencing entry, center, boundary, or pause. We occasion encounters of varied charging qualities through material decisions and interventions conceived and configured to fit with the architectural container.

Claiming the wall area above the elevator doors for ornament as threshold[15] and, decoratively, as architecturally integrated art,[16] we marked the shift between horizontal and vertical movement as a charged element in the experience of the place.

Textured screens announce the passage between the two dimensions as a formal event and make known the movement of people and machines beyond the wall, intentionally recalling intricate cast iron elevator enclosures. Visually ascending and descending, the patterns run vertically and extend the door frames to the ceiling. Their width follows the structure holding the frames, with the ornamented area bound by vertical borders.

In a nod to continuity and community, we used the overlayed configuration of genealogical patterns for the geometry of the decorative field. The orthogonal grid shifts diagonally between the layers to create the shadow systems characteristic of these patterns. (Fig. 5)

Conceived in spatial dialogue with several large, handcrafted globes of metal keys hung above the waiting area in front of the elevators, the screens use compositions of circular solids and voids of relatable scale and the keyhole as a legible trope. The key was identified early in the design process as an important symbol for Canopy's ethos, sparking memories of travel, recalling old hotels and their key cubbies on the wall behind the reception counter. The keyholes build on this association to act symbolically and visually as portals for the imagination, suggesting the promise of unveiling mysteries or perhaps triggering the memory of previous travels. (Fig. 6)

---

14 A design effort in close collaboration with Street-Works Studio.

15 "Human activities are bounded by constraint structures [...] – and entail entrances (as well as exits) from these situated contexts. The tendencies to use ornaments for entrances – framing the surroundings of doors, or doors themselves – are present in architectural spaces in human history. The ornamentation of the entrance can be contrasted with its absence further away from the boundary of the everyday activity that it marks." (Valsiner 2008, 73)

16 As opposed to being an autonomous piece of décor, such as a large map or painting placed in the middle of the wall above the elevators, among alternatives considered.

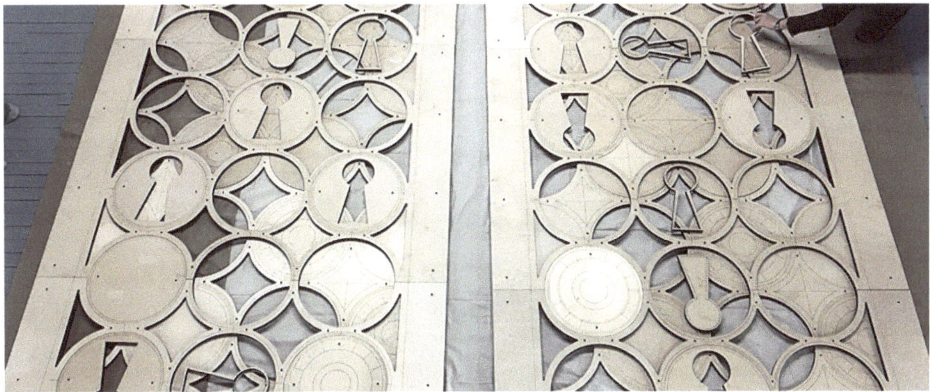

Figure 8

The panels are identical in their base structure. To achieve richness and complexity, we laser-cut layers and individual elements such that we could arrange them by hand in direct interaction with the object. Replacing them in syncopated symmetry operations, we enacted Ruskin's repose of implied causality of action through the deliberate work invested in the making.

Ornamented fields super-position the geometric lattice and the active figure of ornament, energizing the abstract uniformity of the grid with the 'live' element in a harmonious dance of secondary figures in the matrix.[17] The resulting visual energy could range between stillness and hyperactivity, with many possible states of balance and corresponding emotional and affective charge. In our process, we identified one state of visual harmony and balance. We then disrupted the composition with strategic 'accidents' of placement, increasing the tension within the pattern and, consequentially, in the aesthetic experience and energetic charge.[18] While the active figure maintains its integrity within the decorative field and acts at a higher level of perception and association of meaning, its iterations as edge, outline, or border forces it beyond symbol or literal representation, pushing it towards "an abstraction, a fragment or a sensation." (Jespersen 2008. 151)

Circles and radial lines etch the surface for added texture, a secondary element of interest that becomes apparent as one nears the screens; color and fasteners add mass and physical presence in another balancing act between too much and too

---

17 *"In surface decorations, any arrangement of forms [...] consisting only of straight lines, is monotonous, and affords but imperfect pleasure; but introduce lines which tend to carry the eye towards the angles, [...] and you have at once an increased pleasure. Then add lines giving a circular tendency, [...] and you have now complete harmony. In this case the square is the leading form or tonic; the angular and the curved are subordinate." O. Jones explaining the principle of combination in his description of Moorish ornament (1856/2001, p. 190), quoted by Valsiner (Valsiner 2008, 69)*

18 *Most efficient spatial relationships can be imagined: the way a nascent protein finds its final stable shape in milliseconds, folding onto itself into the state of lowest potential energy, the same way a system of interlocking structures may find a most efficient configuration inherent in the spatial nature of the parts. Such a state would correspond to Jones' state of repose as "absence of any want" (Jespersen, 2008, 144). However, increased tension between the parts can be sustained by a complex structure before compromising its structural integrity.*

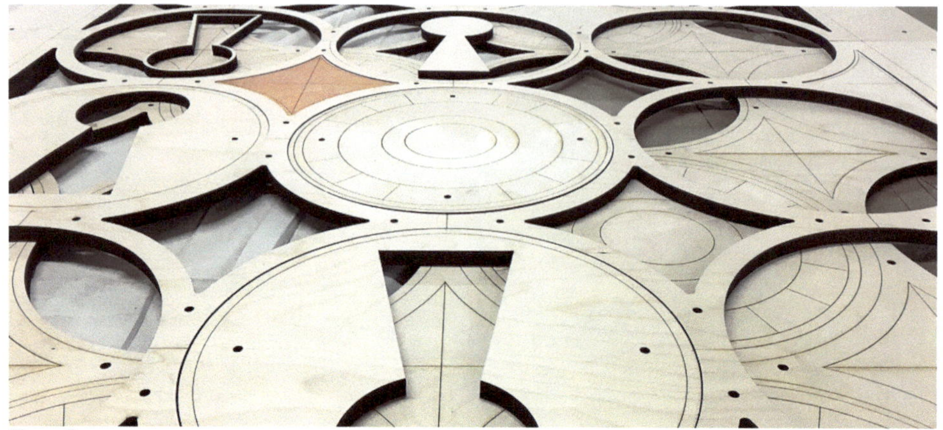
Figure 9

little. Colorful accent inserts appear to have escaped from the landscape of the moss wall, pulsating across the panels. (Fig. 7-10)

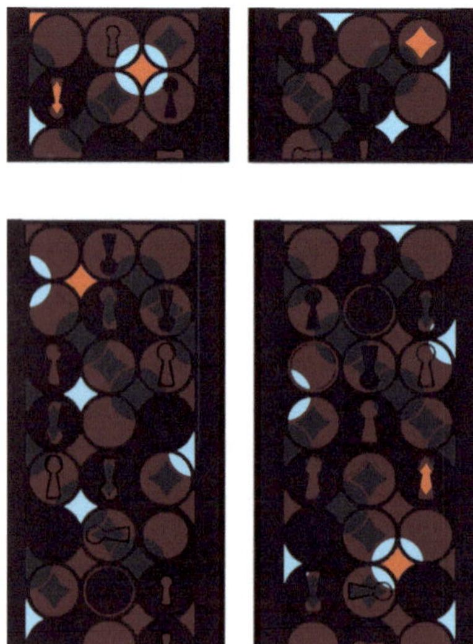
Figure 10

Unlike flat patterns or cutouts, the screens have relief and voids. They are a re-creation, or elaboration, of a flat pattern in three dimensions. The assembly is simultaneously ornament constructed and decorative object integrated into the architecture of the place, intrinsic and extrinsic to the structure it enlivens. (Fig. 11-13) Acting in concert, its form, content, color, space, and light aim at creating Owen Jones' heightened experience of repose, of "spiritual elevation," "a mental feeling, an emotional condition brought about by the satisfaction of both feeling and intellect [...]." (Jespersen 2008, 152)

These experiences of complexity[19] and meaning may not serve 'essential' survival functions, like answering our need for food, sleep, and shelter – functions fulfilled, as it happens, by a well-appointed and comfortable hotel. Yet such experiences entangle our sensations and perceptions and engage us.[20]

---

19 *"Eysenck cites evidence that it is the copresence of simplicity and complexity in a perceived form that excites aesthetic appreciation, but that what counts as simple or complex may depend on personality type..." – one can assume that it depends as well on disposition/state of mind. (Pepperell 2018, 425j)*

20 *"To live day to day is insufficient for human beings; we need to transcend, transport, escape; we need to see overall patterns in our lives. We need hope, a sense of the future. And we need freedom (or the illusion of freedom) to go beyond ourselves... in states of mind which allow us to travel to other worlds, to transcend our immediate surroundings. We need detachment of this sort as much as we need direct engagement in our lives." (Sachs 2013, 90)*

Ornament brings life and pause, joy and wonder. In repose with the ornamented piece, the ornamenter within senses the energy of figures awakening the decorative field and is, in turn, awakened. Story, imagination, and patterns-that-connect create recognitions of particular content and reverberations with universal tropes. In engagement with it, we are simultaneously in the present and beyond it. We experience the universe, the instance, contraction and expansion, contemplative relief, and energetic charge. This activation translates into our being there while being transported, transcending space and time while anchored in them through a memorable experience of place.[21]

References:

Pepperell, Robert. 2018. "Art, Energy and The Brain." in Progress in Brain Research, Volume 237, 417-435. https://doi.org/10.1016/bs.pbr.2018.03.022

Jespersen, John K., "Originality and Jones' The Grammar of Ornament of 1856" (2008). Faculty Publications. Paper 5. http://digitalcommons.ric.edu/facultypublications/5

Bloomer, Kent. 2019 "Ornament and Harbor", T3xture no.4 (2019), 21-29

Bloomer, Kent C., and John Kresten Jespersen. Ph.D. 2015. "Ornament as Distinct from Decoration." T3xture No.2 (2015) 18-35.

Schuster, Carl & Carpenter, Edmund. 1996. "Patterns That Connect: Social Symbolism in Tribal Art". New York: Abrams.

Valsiner, Jaan. 2008, Ornamented Worlds and Textures of Feelings: The Power of Abundance", Critical Social Studies No 1, 67-78.

Sachs, Oliver. 2013. Hallucinations, London: Picador.

Stokes, Mark. 2013. "What Geometric Visual Hallucinations Tell Us about the Visual Cortex", "Brain Metrics", Accessed Nov. 5 2020. https://www.nature.com/scitable/blog/brain-metrics/what_do_hallucinations_tell_us/

"Sensation and Perception", Module 5 in "Introduction to Psychology", Lumen, accessed November 11, 2020 https://courses.lumenlearning.com/wmopen-psychology/chapter/outcome-sensation-and-perception/

Bloomer, Kent C., and John Kresten Jespersen. Ph.D. 2015. "Ornament as Distinct from Decoration." T3xture No.2 (2015) 18-35.
Schuster, Carl & Carpenter, Edmund. 1996. "Patterns That Connect: Social Symbolism in Tribal Art". New York: Abrams.

---

21 The simultaneity of sensorial and perceptual phenomena may possibly be mapped in the cortical and sensorial pathways as they get activated in cascades of charges and/or discharges in brain and body. Be it calming (depressants) or energizing (stimulants), they may find a counterpart in the action and response to drugs. Could the qualities and configurations of these responses find correlations in hallucinatory and imaginary effects? Chemical and electro-magnetic phenomena, integrated in an energy-based approach (as framed by Pepperell in Art, Energy and The Brain) may open new paths for neuroscience to explain the phenomenology of the aesthetic experience – a window into the energies that the making of ornament and the use of hallucinatory drugs strive to harness and actualize across ages and cultures.

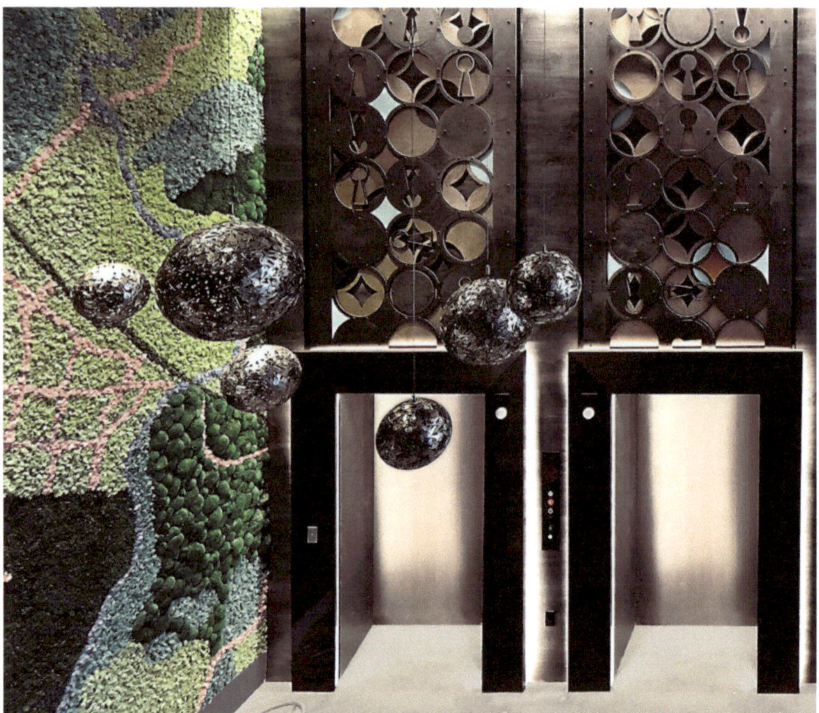

Figure 11

Valsiner, Jaan. 2008, Ornamented Worlds and Textures of Feelings: The Power of Abundance", Critical Social Studies No 1, 67-78.

Sachs, Oliver. 2013. Hallucinations, London: Picador.

Stokes, Mark. 2013. "What Geometric Visual Hallucinations Tell Us about the Visual Cortex", "Brain Metrics", Accessed Nov. 5 2020. https://www.nature.com/scitable/blog/brain-metrics/what_do_hallucinations_tell_us/

"Sensation and Perception", Module 5 in "Introduction to Psychology", Lumen, accessed November 11, 2020 https://courses.lumenlearning.com/wmopen-psychology/chapter/outcome-sensation-and-perception/

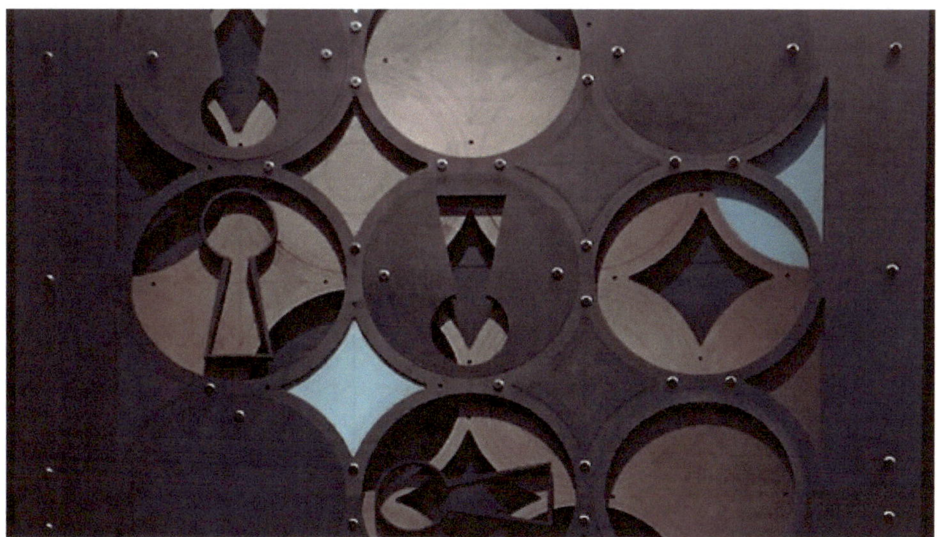

Figure 12

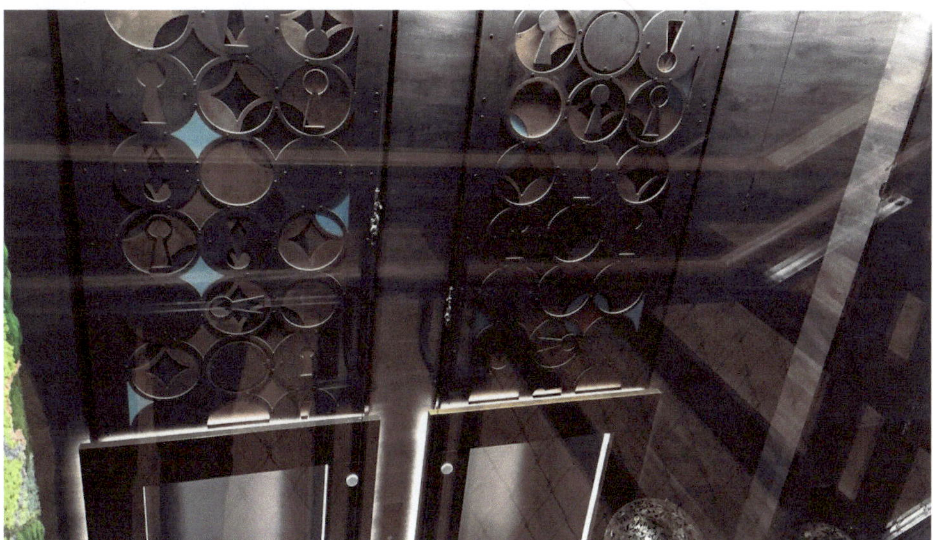

Figure 13

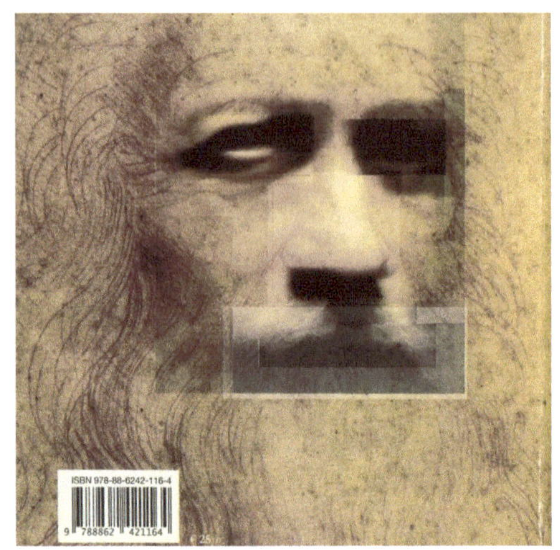

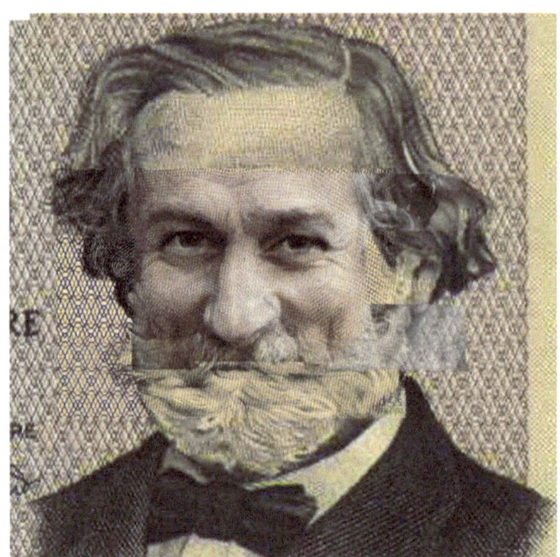

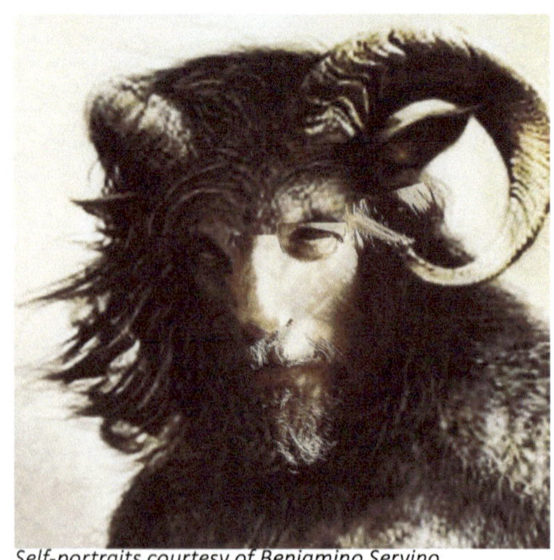

Self-portraits courtesy of Beniamino Servino
Instagram: @beniamino_servino

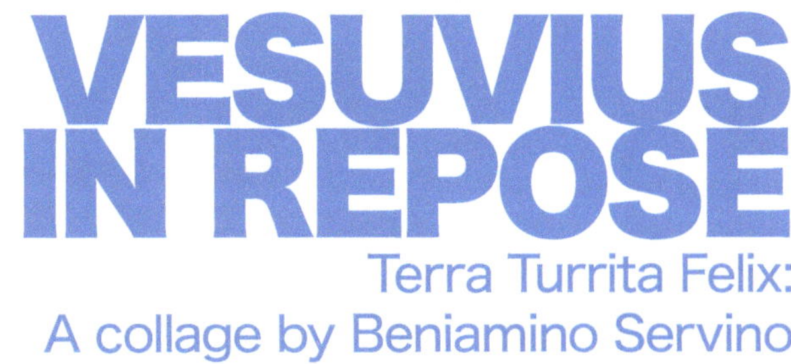

Beniamino Servino, the prolific Italian architect practicing in Caserta, Italy, has established a following with speculative drawings, models, and collages on his eye-popping Instagram page. An email conversation with the mercurial artist, who tends to superimpose his likeness over illustrations of da Vinci and others, led to the comparison of our home cities, Baltimore and Caserta.

While we saw similarities, the differences are stunning. Caserta and Baltimore are both industrial cities in repose—pausing between growth and an unknown future. However, Caserta sits in the shadow of the active volcano, Vesuvius. The residents of Caserta live in the shadow of Vesuvius, an active volcano that last erupted in 1944. So, we asked him,

"what is life like living near a volcano in repose—one that may awaken at any moment?"

In our exchange, we shared a painting, "A English Garden in Caserta," by the artist, Jacob Philipp Hackert, depicting Vesuvius and Caserta with an English garden in the foreground. Servino responded with cylindrical interventions imposed on the volcano landscape in the collage on pages 22 and 23.

What are these enormous drums? He won't say.

In some of Servino's illustrations, he describes similar forms as telescopes. We think they may be influenced by Casertan castles? But then again, volcanic vents come to mind. We wonder, are they vessels to be programmed with future uses? Are they reflections of the many sides of Caserta, nature, pattern, ornament, industry?

By studying Servino's telescopes, we daydream about his intent and try to understand the man behind the illustrations. Did he create them solely for our amusement, or does he intend a greater purpose?

The maestro leaves it for us to determine.

Those who dwell in Vesuvius' surrounding lands and cities must monitor the crater's rim, anticipating the end of its repose.

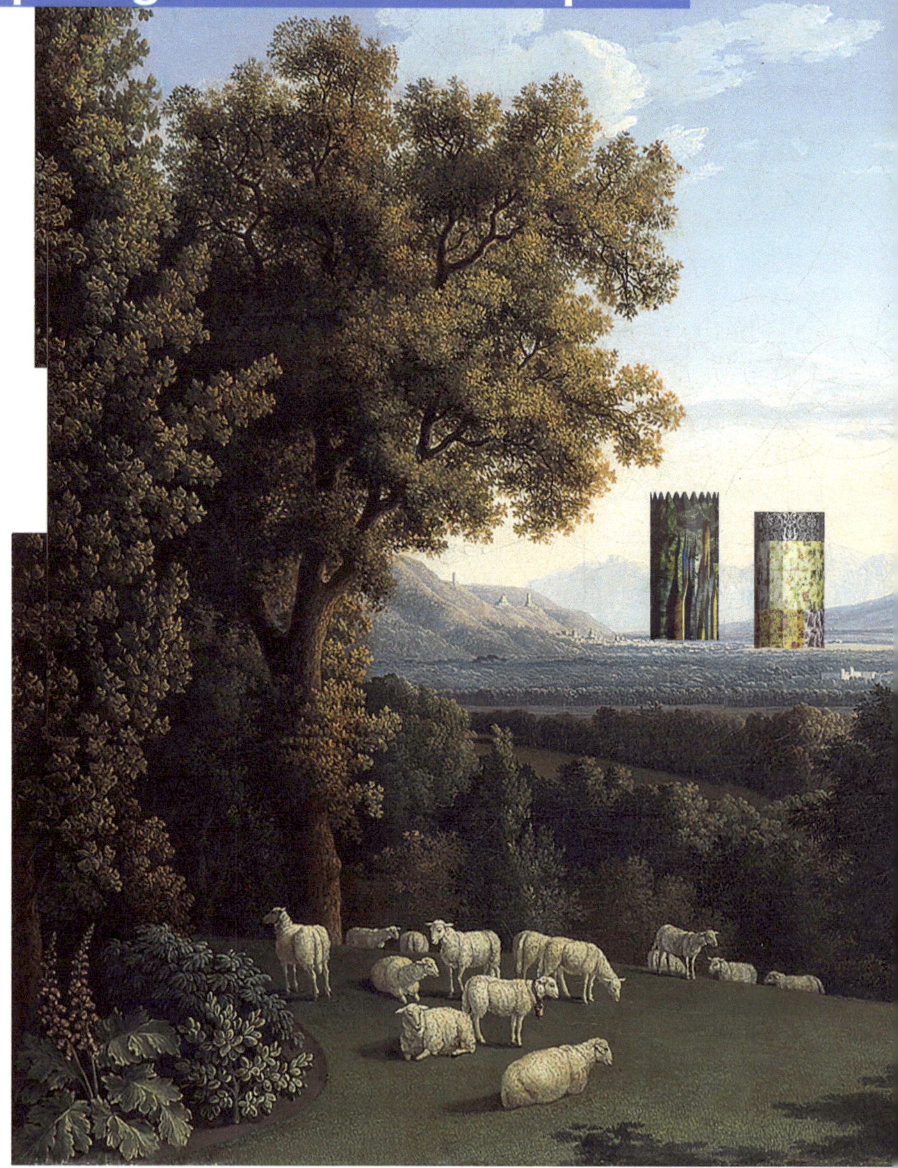

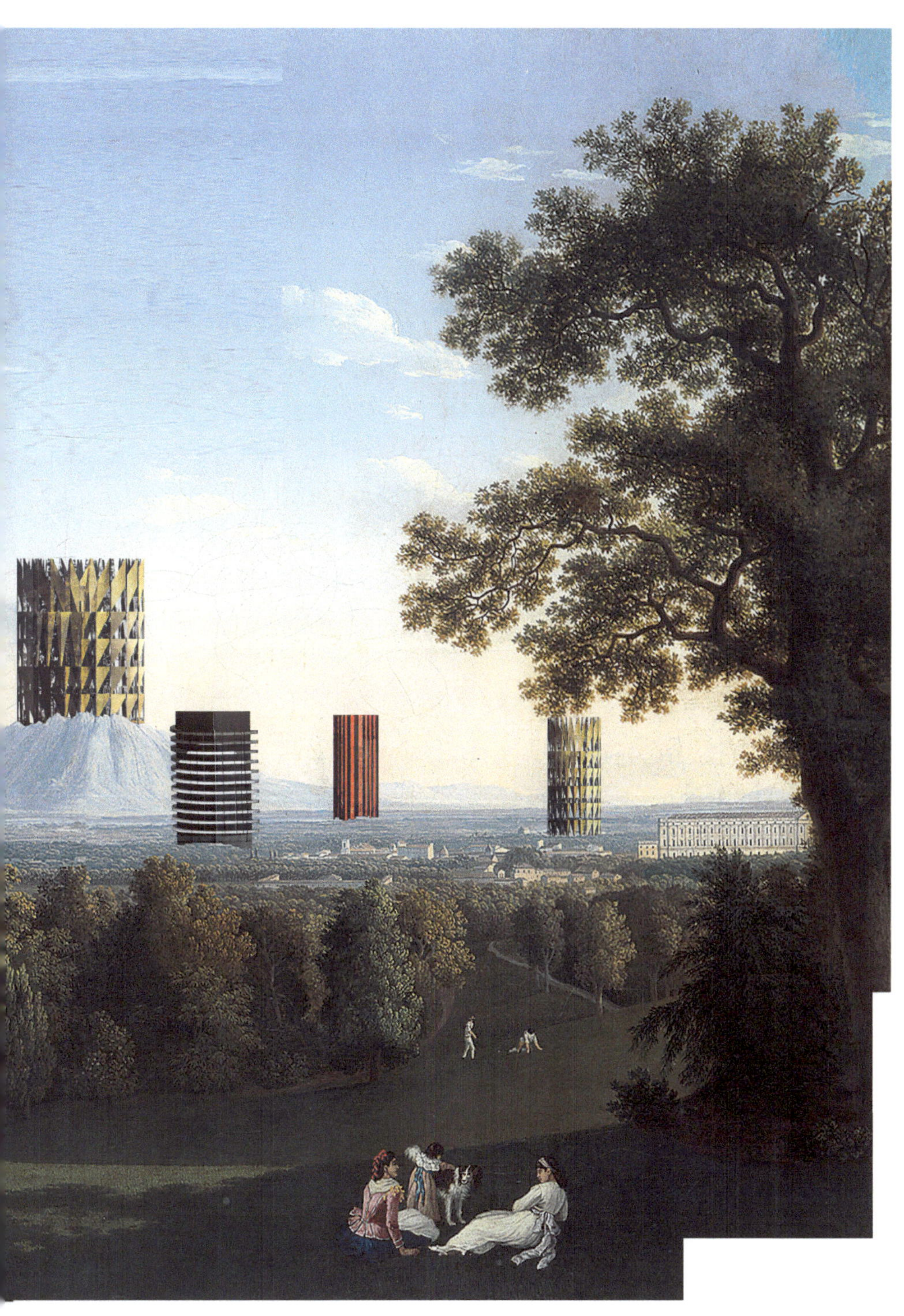

"LIKE THE LIVING BRAIN THE MIND, ESPECIALLY WHEN EXPERIENCING ART, IS ACTUALIZED, EVER MOVING, RICHLY DIFFERENTIATED, INTEGRATED, AND MARKED BY MYRIAD STATES OF TENSION. IT IS WORKING TO KEEP US ALIVE AND, AT ITS BEST, FEELING ALIVE."

"LIFE IS A SPECIAL FORM OF ENERGY, MIND IS A SPECIAL FORM OF LIFE, AND ART IS A SPECIAL FORM OF MIND."

IOANA BARAC

RISING UNITY

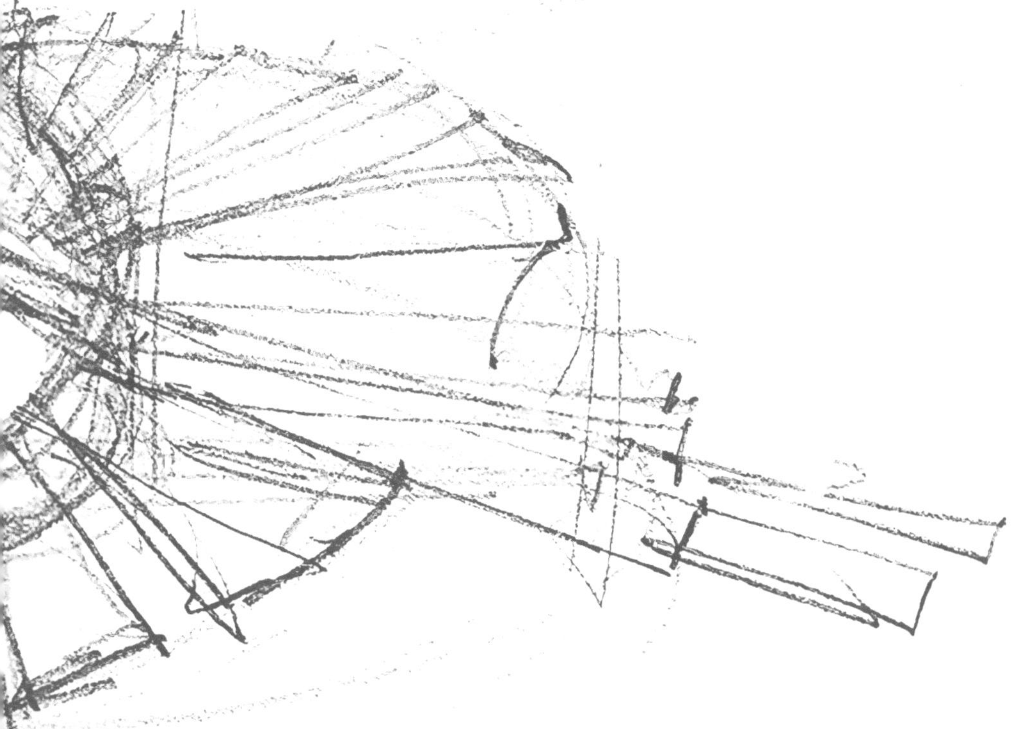

When we say that an artwork moves us, we mean we are changed by the encounter, by the experience of being in the presence and in full awareness of the piece of art. The interaction with the object in the external spatial and temporal reality is mirrored in the space-time fabric of the imagination. The change initiated by the visual reception – the electro-magnetic energy of light reaching the eye, precipitating electrochemical activity in the visual cortex – cascades in changes of our state of mind and body. Layers of explicit and implicit meaning, inherent in the object or inferred subjectively, elicit "perceptual and cognitive tensions". These, Pepperell writes, mean "experiencing the dynamic "being-at-work" (ενέργεια) of art."

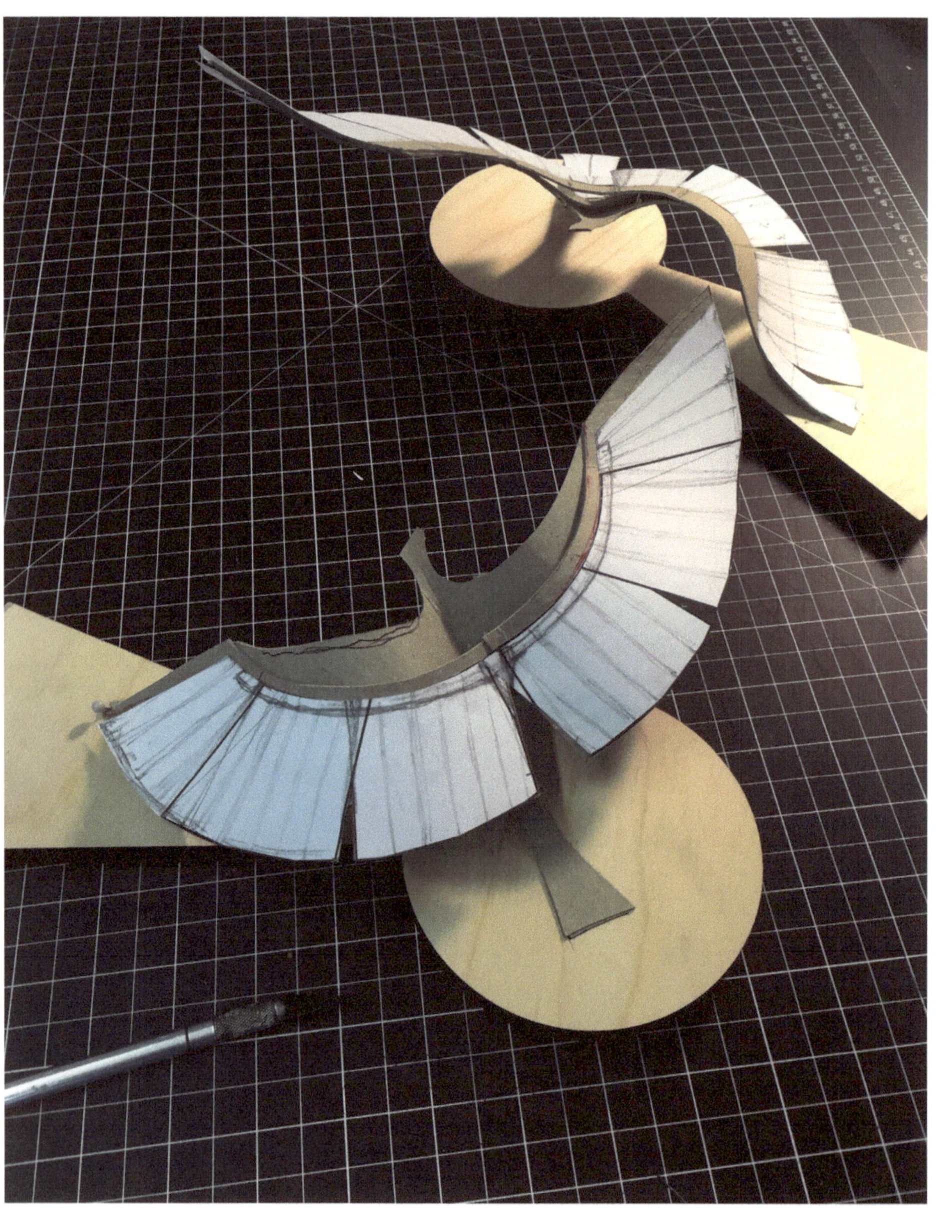

THE ENERGIES OF RISING UNITY:

1. Embedded energy: in the making of ? actualized? the work?
   - the extraction raw materials; geology and man
   - the modified materials and parts; human and machine fabrication
   - the writing and printing
   - the assembling of the sculpture: human work and intent
   - the attachment to the stand; the fasteners
   - hand-made: is that legible? If yes, does it add value? Is that 'the energy of life' we respond to?

2. Potential energy? Tension – in the curves; in the mechanical bonds; chemical bonds;
   - (how visible is this?)
   - in the material – Mass as energy
   - in the curved wings and overlay
   - overall shape
   - gravity
   - in the connections

3. Received/borrowed Energy: Light: external, received, reflected.
   - Is what makes the object visible in the first place
   - The quality of the surface finish Accentuating surfaces shapes
   - Reflecting – inserting in the object external content and energy
   - Translucency

4. Kinetic energy: Literal: Movement of parts (also received and potential, categories overlap)
   - Feathers, free to flutter
   - Wings, oscillating if pressed, touched
   - Overall mobility (nomad sculpture plus pedestal)

5. Content: activating? intellectual energy? Mental? Rational; 'superior cortex' (as configuration)
   - bird - phoenix
   - signatures
   - flight
   - wound
   - re-birth, legend
   - mirror

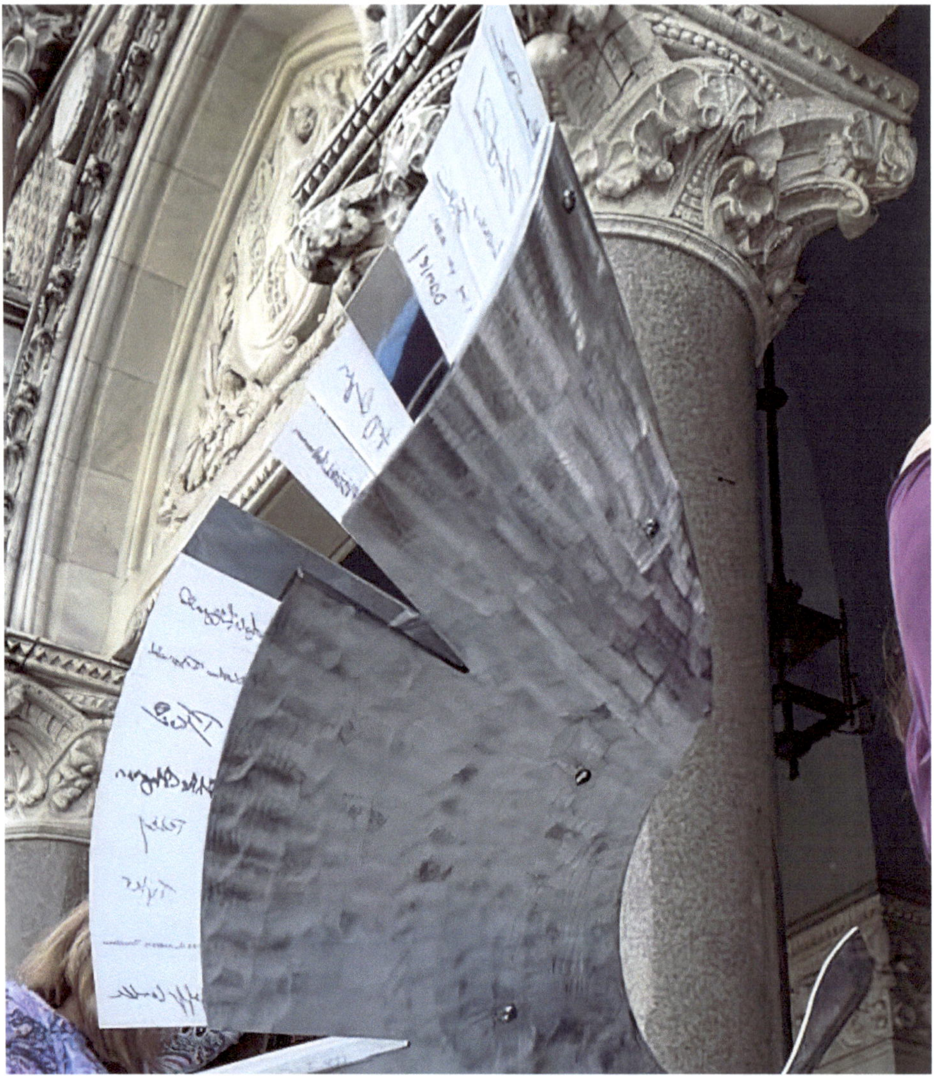

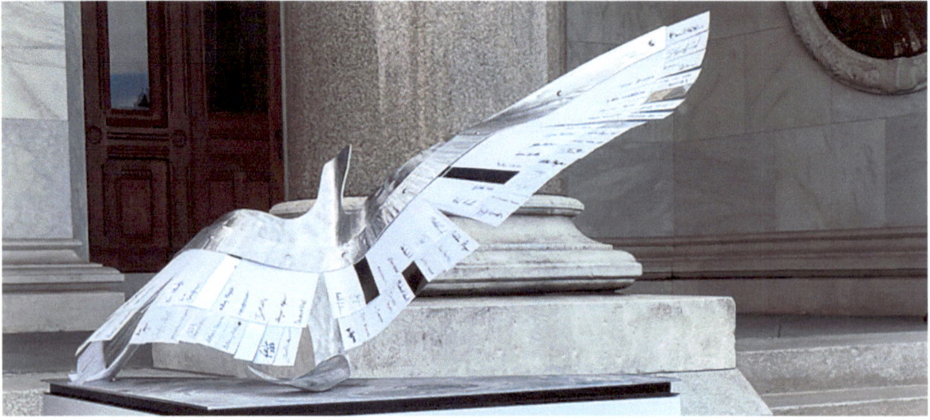

6. Emotional energy: relating content and feelings, rational and irrational, intellectual and instinctive
    - Death
    - Precarious balance
    - Appearance of movement – implied imbalance or action
    - Appearance of growth
    - Recognition of life
    - Sense of loss
    - Sense of transcendence
    - Sense of flow

7. Life energy - Meaning and the aesthetic experience
    - What makes one want to keep living
    - Purpose, patterns, direction
    - Simultaneity of perception; synchronized 'arrival' of the neuronal transmission
    - Discharge (lightning rod) – in patterns and tandems

Many kinds of encounters affect us, move us. When we create a piece of art, we aim at certain effects – to change a certain way; moreover, we mean for the change to last.

The longing for more captured in this particular sculpture is the need to transcend, to fly; to leave the earth, to find meaning, connection, to escape...

To be remembered as rising, not falling, both in aspiration and in consequence – a reconsideration of the past and future purpose.

To energize the moment and the future.

To heal, too – to give meaning to the past, include it in the continuum past-present-future.

Note: The Project was a Traveling Memorial Sculpture for Victims of Opioid Overdose. It was commissioned by Demand Zero & For Cameron and realized by Atelier Cue in 2020.

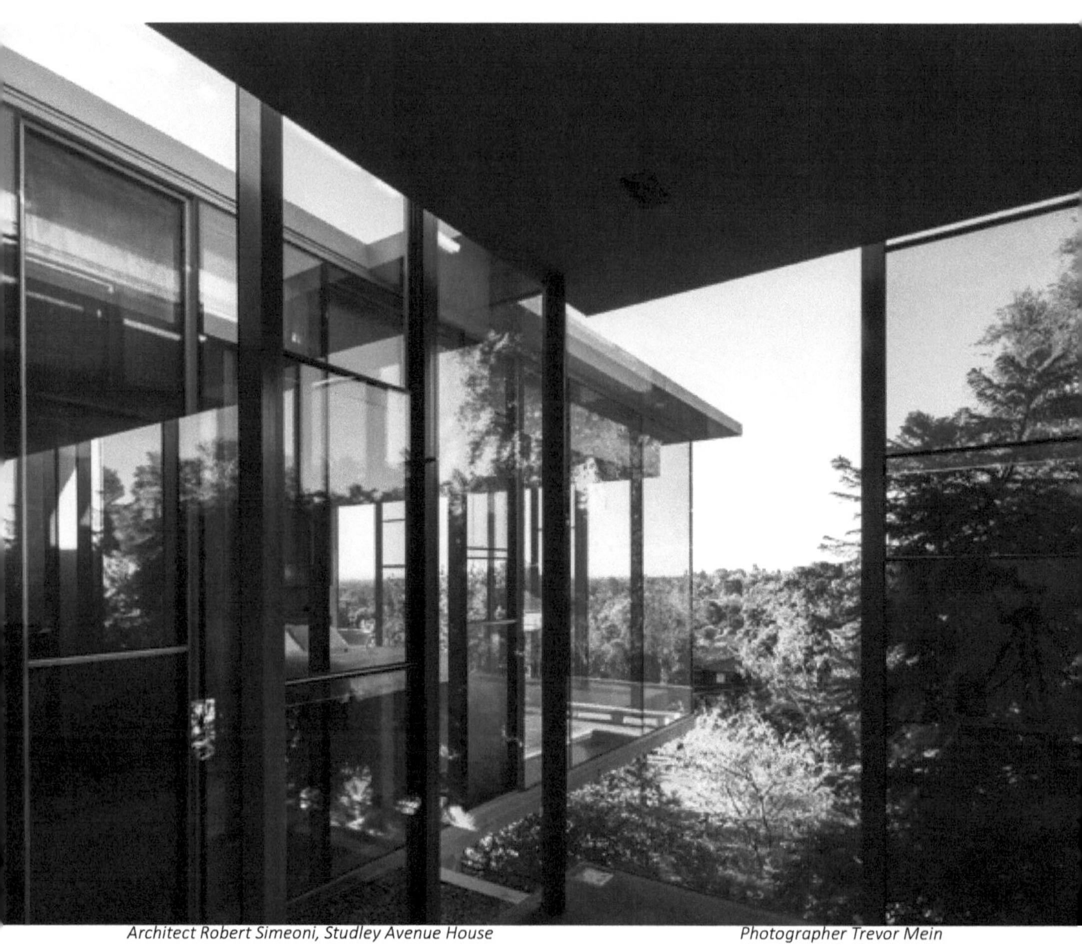

Architect Robert Simeoni, Studley Avenue House *Photographer Trevor Mein*

A DESIGN SOLUTION FOR WARTIME MATERIAL SHORTAGES AND THE DESIRE FOR FAMILIES TO BE CLOSE TO ONE ANOTHER AFTER THE TRAUMA OF WAR, OPEN PLAN LIVING HAS PROVIDED FREEDOM, LIGHT, AND COMMUNION FOR MORE THAN A CENTURY. IS THAT WHAT WE NEED NOW?

HAS OUR LOVE AFFAIR WITH OPEN-PLAN LIVING FINALLY ENDED?

After months of lockdowns during the worldwide COVID-19 pandemic, our residential realization has become a cause for consideration. It is challenging to find moments of repose when there is little privacy or separation of spaces at home. These moments of silence are essential as they counterbalance the energy required to cope in these testing times. Our world seems so far removed from the idealized version of Pierre Koenig's 1960 Stahl House, a most iconic striking example of open-plan modernism, a perfect balance between the building's bold, cantilevered exterior and chic, comfortable interior.

Time Magazine has called Koenig's Los Angeles house "the most successful real estate image ever taken," stating it perpetuates the "American Dream." An ethos for freedom, prosperity, and success.
This image is both beguiling and beautiful. The perfect balance of repose and energy. Impressive with its complicated engineering and careful placement of the corner aspect over a clifftop. To survey a stylish scene of serene sympathies empowers one to believe in this dream—a vision for a bygone era.

An epoch when people worked nine to five in offices, schedules strictly delineated days; it was impossible to work from home. The twenty-four-hour clock was something only Wall Street stockbrokers and spacemen acknowledged. The home served fewer functions. It was a place for rest, relaxation, privacy, domestic duties, and dinner parties. Today the house has many more functions. For large numbers of people, it has become a workplace, educational facility, and hospice (hospital in the home), placing more pressure on a century-old design. COVID-19 lock downs have forced families to spend months on end with one another. The many parts of ourselves that we share with others have collided

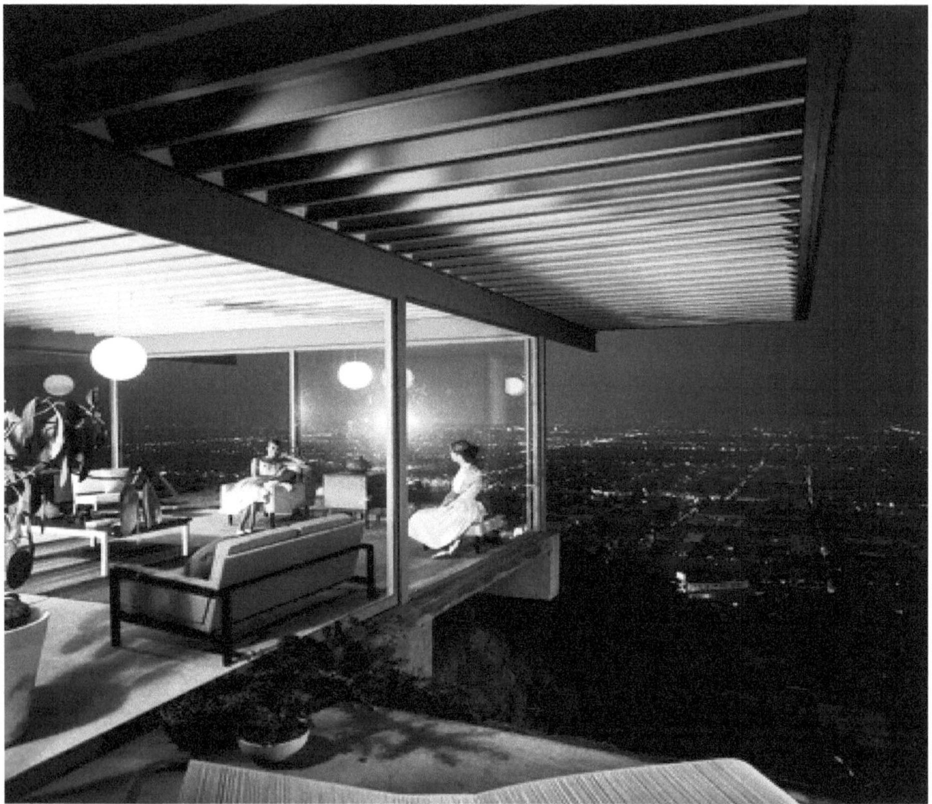

Architect Pierre Koenig *Photographer: Julius Shulman*

into one dimension. There is little separation between self and the space we occupy. The people we work with can now look into our private lives via a screen. The freedom and democracy that informed open-plan design can no longer be maintained. Modern architecture leaves some of us feeling trapped within this transparency.

It was a world event that triggered the open-plan design; it came from the calamity of war. One of the first explicit formulations of the open-plan as a universal principle came from Swiss architect and polemicist Le Corbusier in the 1920s; he coined the term "le plan libre," the free plan a five-point manifesto published in 1927. The key to it was pilotis (columns) instead of load-bearing walls. Corridors became obsolete. Large expanses of glass became synonymous with streamlined modernist designs.

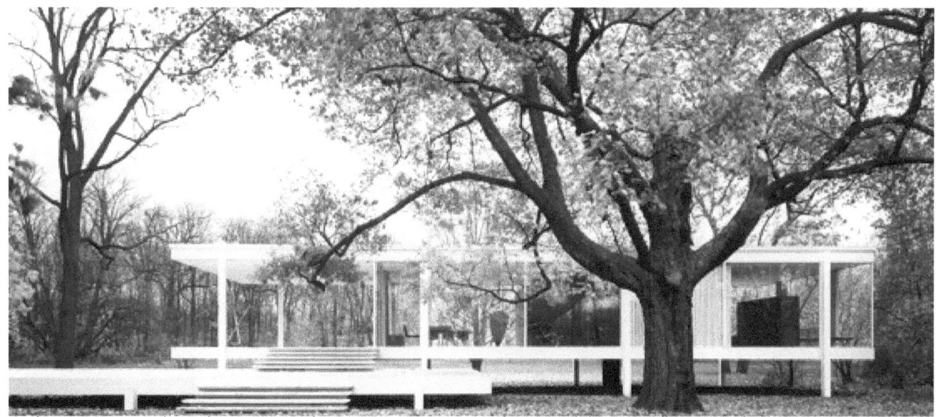

Architect Mies van der Rohe, Farnsworth House *Photograph by Jon Miller, Hedrich Blessing*

Many houses became iconic markers for what it was to be snatched (hip) in the sixties, from Ludwig Mies van der Rohe's slimline Farnsworth House in Illinois (1951) to Frank Lloyd Wright's Neils House in Minneapolis (1951). A period when the usual tension between freedom and safety did not exist, people were liberated from the fear of war.

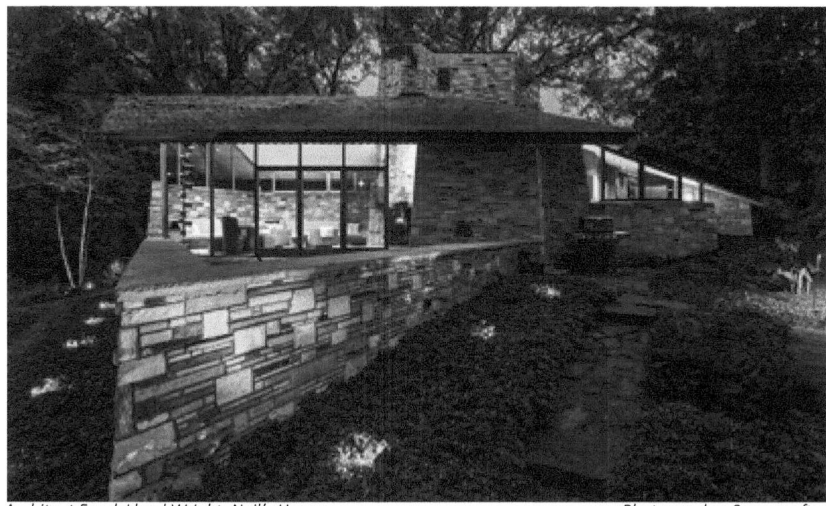

Architect Frank Lloyd Wright, Neil's House *Photographer Spacecraft*

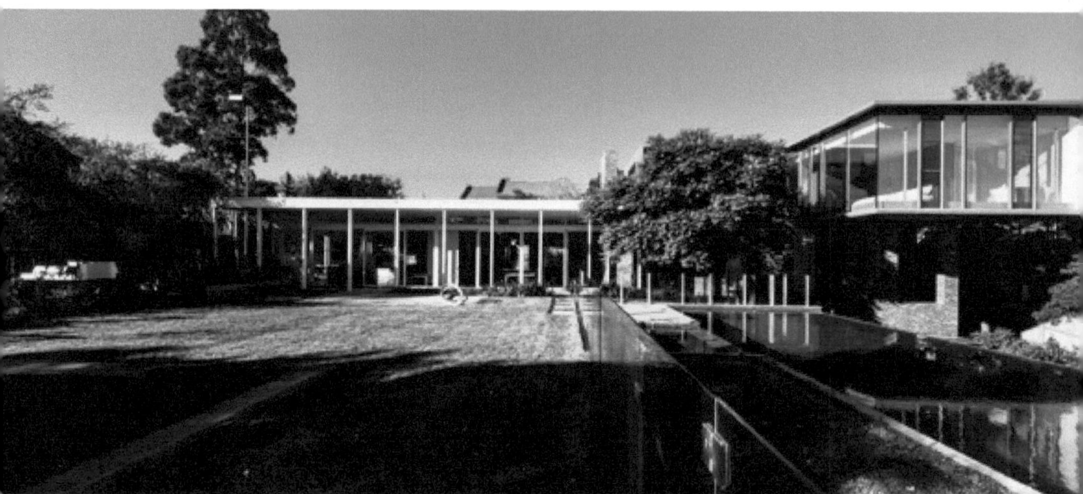

Architect Robert Simeoni, Studley Avenue House. *Photographer: Trevor Mein*

Wright pioneered open plan living in the US with his most famous house, Fallingwater, built-in 1939, portraying his concept of 'organic' architecture. Later Wright built Neil's House, which boasts a post-war Usonian architectural design. A term assigned by Wright referring to a group of around sixty middle-income family homes designed by the architect himself that were affordable and typically small, single-story open-plan dwellings. The homes imparting a feeling of weightlessness, as though one is floating between the interior and exterior, a seamless blend of nature and nurture. Perfect for this moment in time.

In 1958 French philosopher Gaston Bachelard wrote a book; The Poetics of Space. It explores our relationship to architecture in context of the "lived experience" He states in small corners we re-discover darkness, peace, and regeneration." He talks about dreams and repose of interiority, a deeply rooted form of being. The idea of privacy being juxtaposed to open plan is omnipresent at this time. But this concept of open plan was not just a trend, it quickly swept the world and has remained at the forefront of design for decades.

Australia's love affair with the open-plan also continued to be sine qua non. Much like our European and American counterparts, we too appreciated the economies of simplicity and the free-form open spaces. Prominent modernist homes built by mid-century architects sat majestically in the Australian suburban landscape.

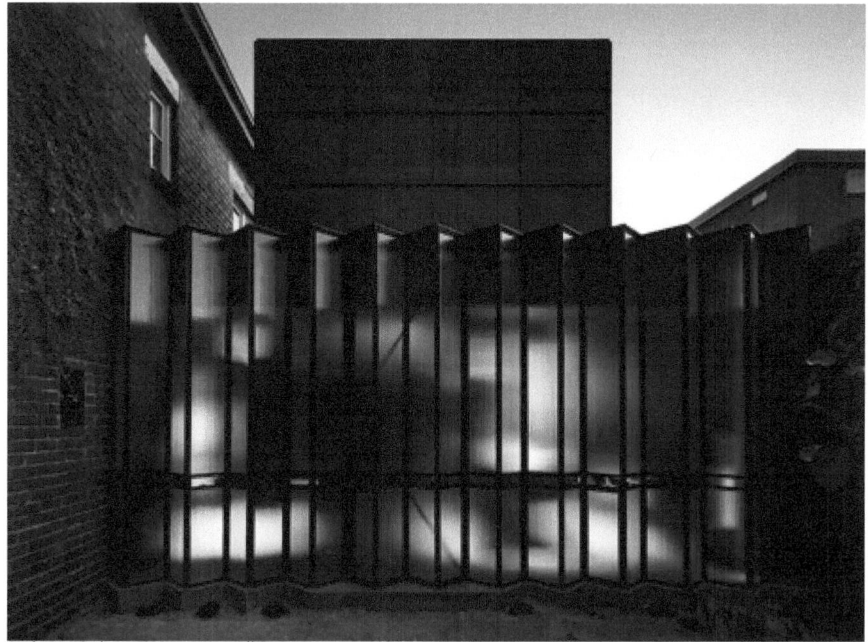

Architect Robert Simeoni, Powell Street House. *Photographer: Derek Swalwell*

"Modern architecture leaves some of us feeling trapped within this transparency."

One such home, the Studley Avenue House, has had the gentle touch of two awarded architects. Originally designed by architect Guilford Bell and then extended by architect Robert Simeoni in 2015. At this time, the desire to preserve and develop the open-plan remained—the new addition of a glass box cantilevered over the pool, a supposition of timeless serenity. The update also incorporated a series of smaller interstitial spaces of indeterminate scale. Simeoni says, "the ad hoc quality of fellow space denotes intimacy."

A moment to reclaim repose.

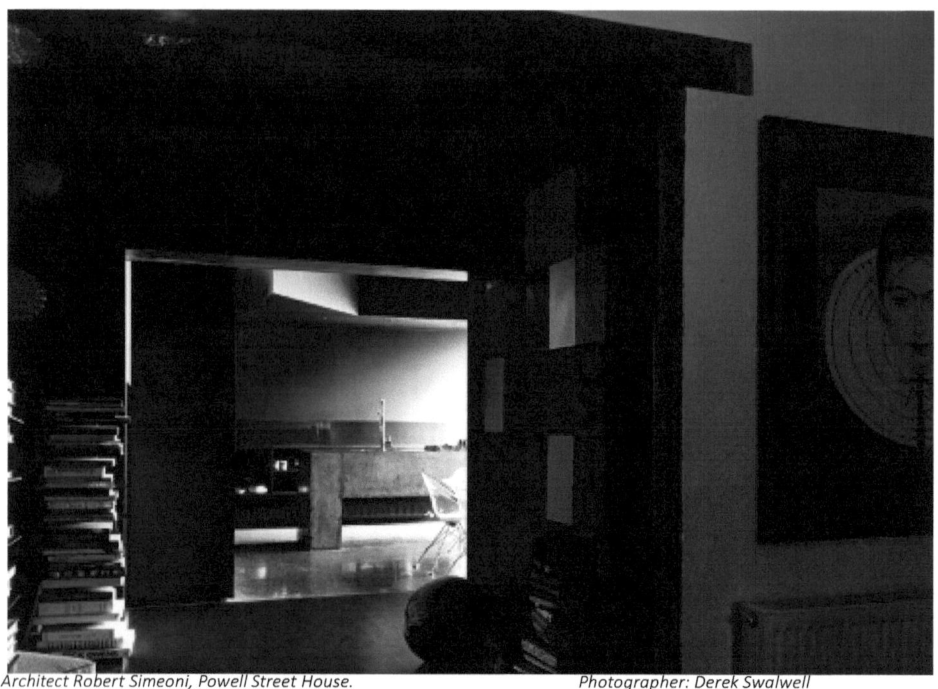

Architect Robert Simeoni, Powell Street House. *Photographer: Derek Swalwell*

When I explore the hypothesis of open-plan being over, Simeoni can quickly contextualize his thoughts. He speaks to the internationally awarded Powell Street house completed in 2019. This existing 1930's duplex comprised a ground floor and first-floor apartment. The owners wished to unite these two dwellings to form a single residence. The new design does not destroy the back, and there are no large panes of glass, the standard treatment for home alterations, with the goal of an open plan. Therefore, I perceive the completed Powell Street house as an iconoclastic declaration that the open plan is dead. But that is not how architect Simeoni reads the interventions undertaken.

"Simeoni says corridors have a reverberative quality, and inadvertent things happen in corridors."

The design was developed with deliberate quietness and a long diagonal aspect through the existing shallow floor plan. Simeoni says this glimpse defers a new suggested view, an implied sense of containment, with a release. A refined interpretation of the open-plan where we can observe how architecture intersects with the interior of a private dwelling and how this relates to the outer world. Creating an opportunity for the inhabitant to curate how much or little is observed by others.

What about the notion of corridors being obsolete? Simeoni says corridors have a reverberative quality, and inadvertent things happen in corridors.' And then I am lost; my mind wanders away, to memories in corridors.

People's lives unfold in buildings, and architecture provokes metaphysical reactions in both the architect and the inhabitant, such as feelings, thinking, and memories. Architecture becomes a form of truth-telling. Living through a pandemic has been challenging for many people, and individual circumstances limit our place in the trajectory of this timeline. I keep returning to a quote by French philosopher Henri Bergson, "The pure present is an ungraspable advance of the past devouring the future." And so, by the time we understand this moment in time, it will have passed. While we seek repose and energy in our everyday existence, open-plan living continues to be part of the chaos.

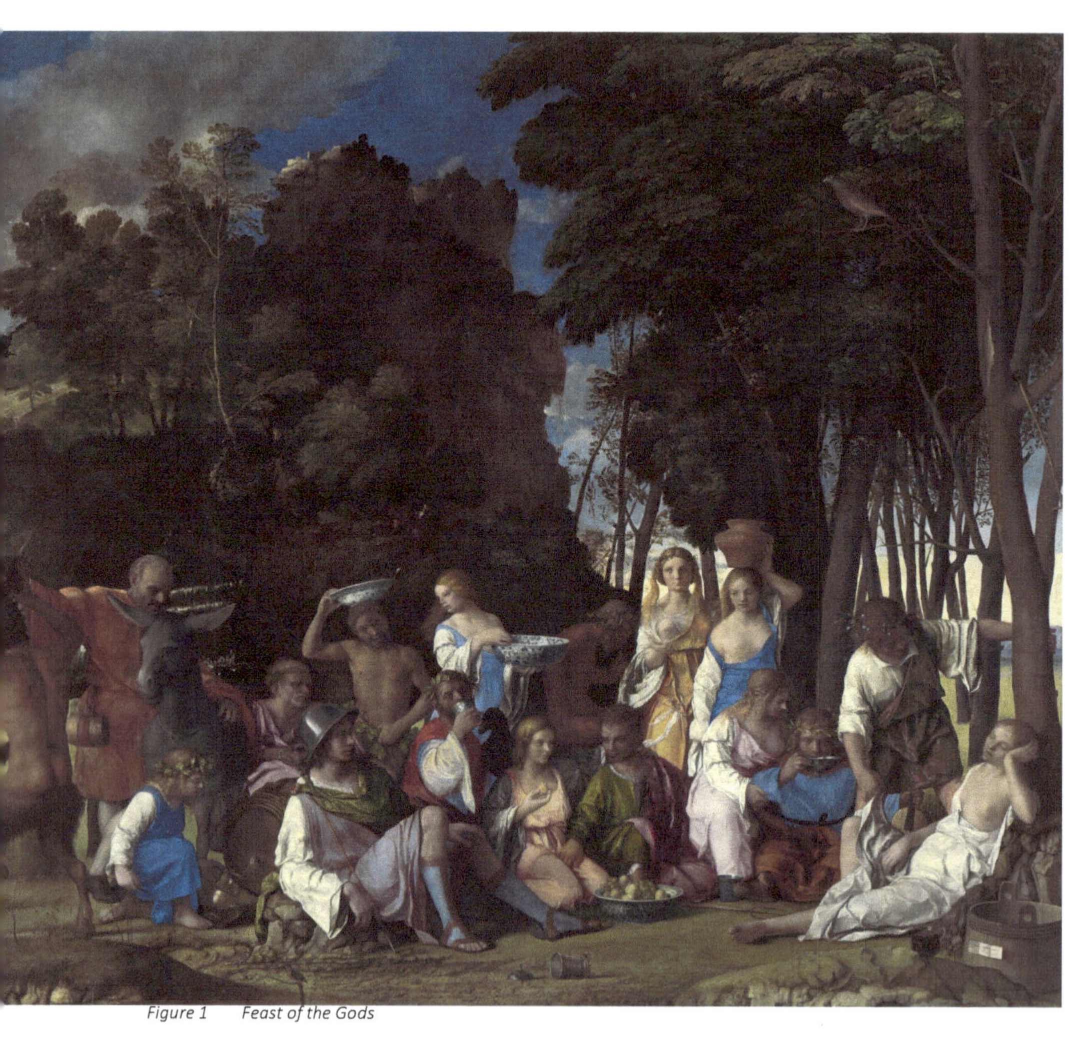

Figure 1 Feast of the Gods

MIRIAM GUSEVICH

URBAN PENTIMENTO:

stories of repose, repentance, and repair.

The COVID-19 pandemic has forced repose on us. Racial injustice calls for repentance. The fragility of our democracy and the threat of global warming warn us to stop and repair.

Repose is a moment of stasis; it is value-neutral. It is charged with value by the human condition. Repose can be oppressive when imposed against our will, under lockdown. Yet repose is a gift. Physiologically, rest and sleep renew nature daily and seasonally; psychologically, repose is a moment of contemplation of prayer; it offers solace and wisdom.

In art, repose is a common theme. Bellini's "The Feast of the Gods" (1514/1529) presents the Gods in repose at a wedding party. It portrays a moment of suspense in Ovid's satire when Silenus' donkey brays and wakes up Lotis, the nymph of chastity, which pushes the virile Priapus away to the merriment of the inebriated Gods. (Fig 1).

Repose is also a process. As we repose and contemplate the painting closely, we can discern puzzling *pentimenti*: dresses under naked breasts, ghostly ruins of temples through the clouds, or a hand moving on the thigh.

Pentimenti in Art are the details effaced by the painter as they repent, later revealed when the oil paint becomes translucent with age. Pentimento refers to the moment of repose, reassessment, and regret before the artist's repainting. There are two stories: repose of the Gods represented in the painting and repose and repentance of the painter revealed by the pentimenti.

Pentimenti are treasured clues to the individual artist's creative process. This painting reveals a more complex story. Modern x-rays and infrared photography,

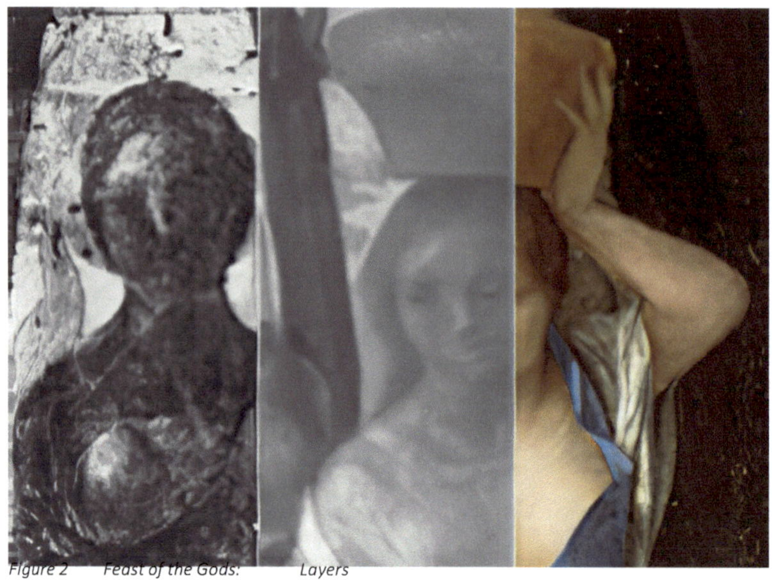
Figure 2 Feast of the Gods: Layers

plus extensive archival research, have confirmed three distinct layers: by Giovanni Bellini (1430/1435 – 1516), Dosso Dossi (1490 – 1542), and Titian (1488 – 1576). (Fig 2)

In this instance, the motivation for the changes was not reflective, it was transactional. The patron, Alfonso d'Este (1486-1534), duke of Ferrara, commissioned the painting, chose the risqué subject, and requested the changes to suit his fancy. He first asked Bellini, who typically painted Madonnas, to spice it up, and he revealed the nymphs' breasts. After Bellini died, he commissioned Dossi, the court painter, to decorate the room, and Dossi painted over Bellini's landscape to fit his decoration. In 1529, Alfonso commissioned Titian, a student of Bellini, to do three more paintings for his studiolo. Titian covered Dossi's addition with a dark, steep mountain against a deep ultramarine sky to match his other paintings for the room. We may regret Dossi's changes to Bellini's original masterpiece, yet the final version is flawed and more profound.

In Western art, artistic changes were concealed, and the pentimento revealed them by accident. In contrast, *Kintsugi* in Japanese art repairs the accident, celebrates the cracks and mends to tell the object's story. Kintsugi is an artistic practice inspired by *Wabi-sabi*, the Japanese philosophy that appreciates the beauty that is flawed and imperfect.

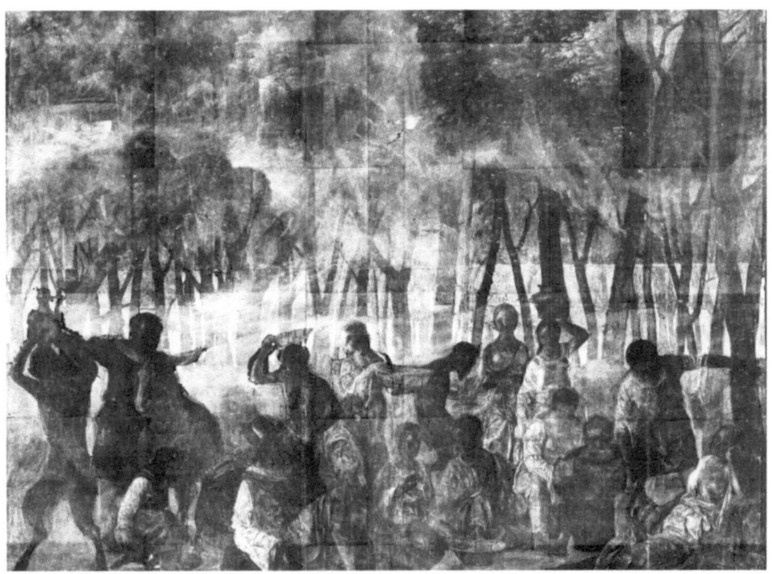

Figure 3 Feast of the Gods: X-Ray

Urban Pentimento

We invoke pentimento and kintsugi in art for inspiration at the environmental scale. Landscapes tell stories. We stop and listen to the people and the site's history.

If landscapes tell stories, the sites of these two projects in Kyiv are profound tragedies. Done in collaboration with Jay Kabriel, these two competitions were meaningful. As a child of the Cuban Revolution, growing up under communism, the events of Euro-Maidan in Central Kyiv brought my sympathy to the Ukrainian people. As the grandchild of Holocaust victims, Babyn-Yar made me confront my family's sorrow.

Constellations (2015)

In Ukraine, Maidan is the public square, the setting of viche, a public assembly where citizens come together to be free. Euro-Maidan was the pro-Europe popular uprising of 2013-2014 against the pro-Russian oligarch. The Heavenly Hundred are the martyrs of Euro-Maidan.

The plan of each crime scene tagged each victim. (fig 4)

We interpreted this document as a pentimento hat revealed the traces of martyrs and links of the Maidans in central Kyiv as patterns of constellations. Metaphorically, like the stars in the sky, each martyr was a star for dignity, and each Maidan was a civic star for freedom. (Fig 5).
In our master plan, a new sacred path weaved the sites of martyrs and Maidans into a new civic constellation of memory and redemption to commemorate their sacrifice. (fig 6) This sacred path connects the sacred and sacrifice, the traces of

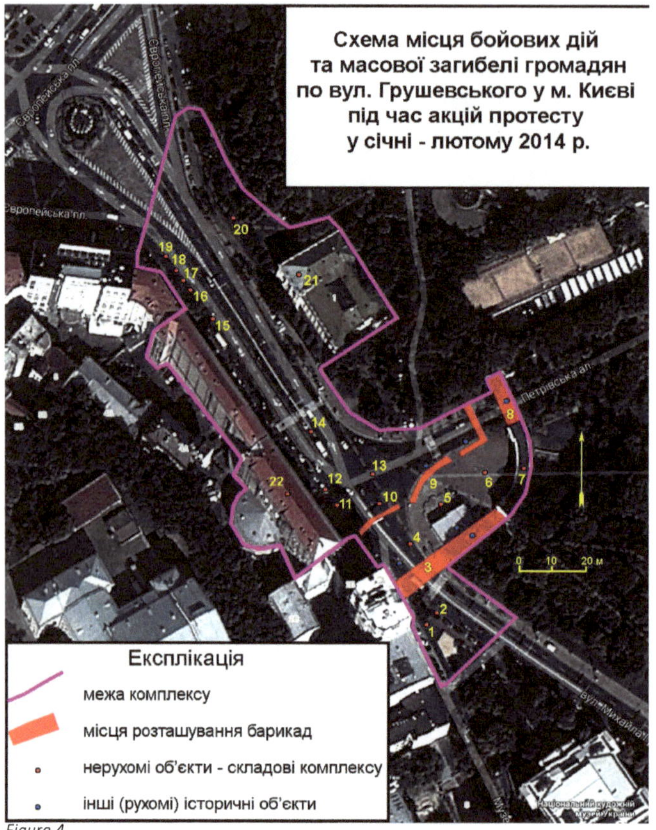

Figure 4

casualties, and the main assembly areas: Maidan Nezalezhnosti- Independence Square (Fig 7) and European Square. It is meant to inspire private meditation and public processions along the most significant Euro-Maidan events.

Clusters of stars mark the sites of martyrdom, and straight lines connect them into "constellations," emanating a soft light. (Fig. 7, 8, 9). The "stars" are clusters of luminescent beads set in the historic black stone pavers: the luminous surface picks up sunlight in the daytime and releases it at night. In the winter, radiant heating at each "star" melts the snow. Finally, we marked the traces of the barricades to define smaller spaces for family memorials and stops along the procession.

Yahtzeit Candles. (2016)

If landscapes tell stories, Babyn-Yar, the grandmother's ravine in Kyiv, Ukraine, is a profound tragedy. It is the most infamous "Holocaust by Bullets" site: on 29–30 September 1941, during Rosh Hashana, the holiest day in the Jewish calendar,

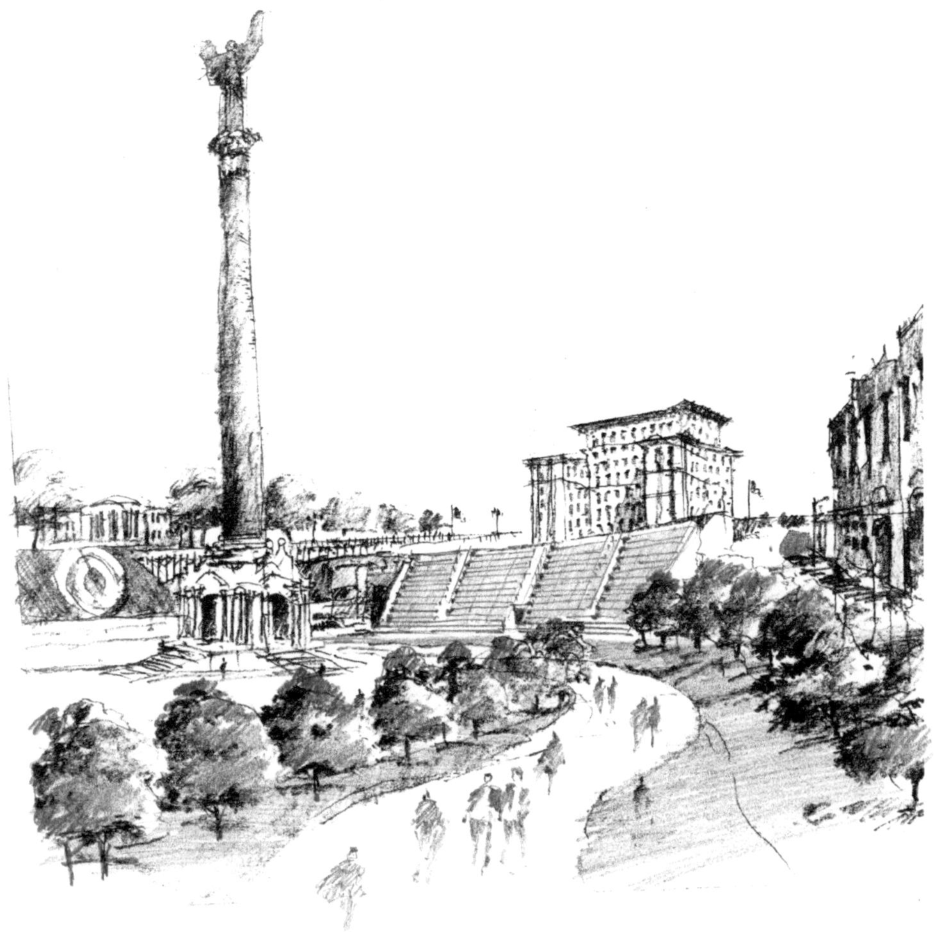

Figure 7

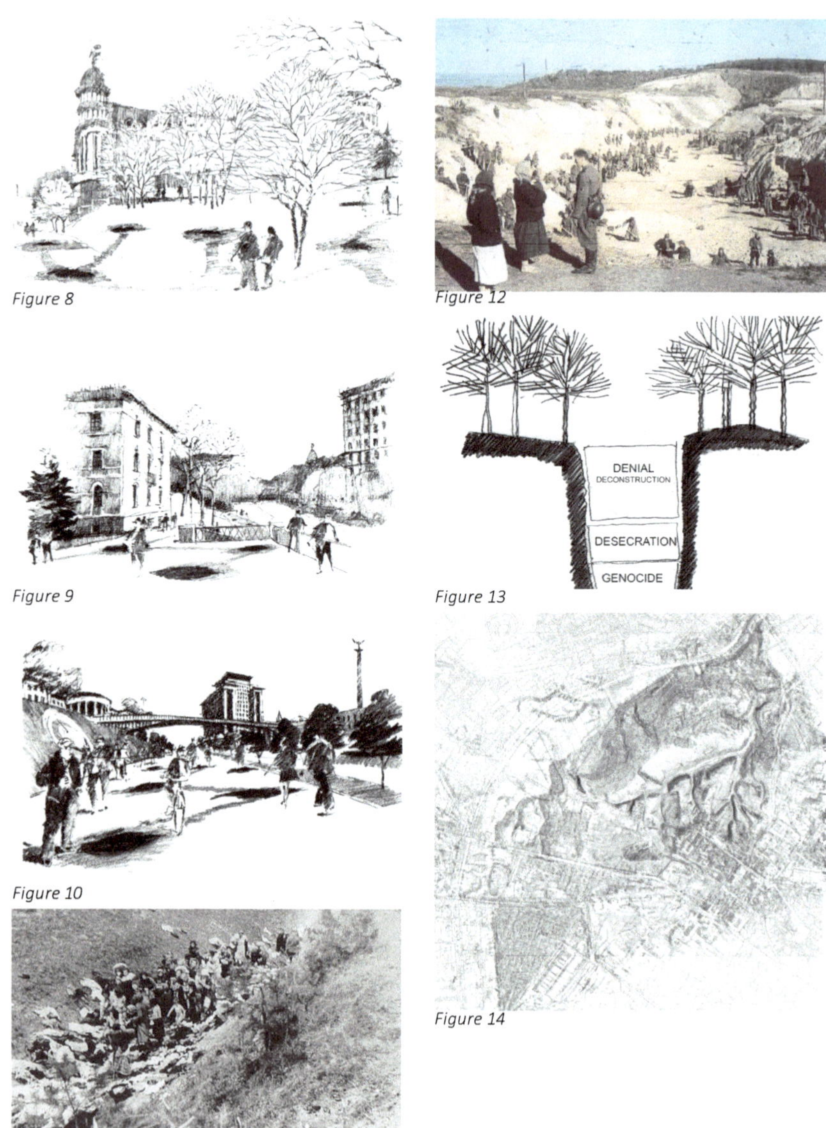

Figure 8

Figure 9

Figure 10

Figure 11

Figure 12

Figure 13

Figure 14

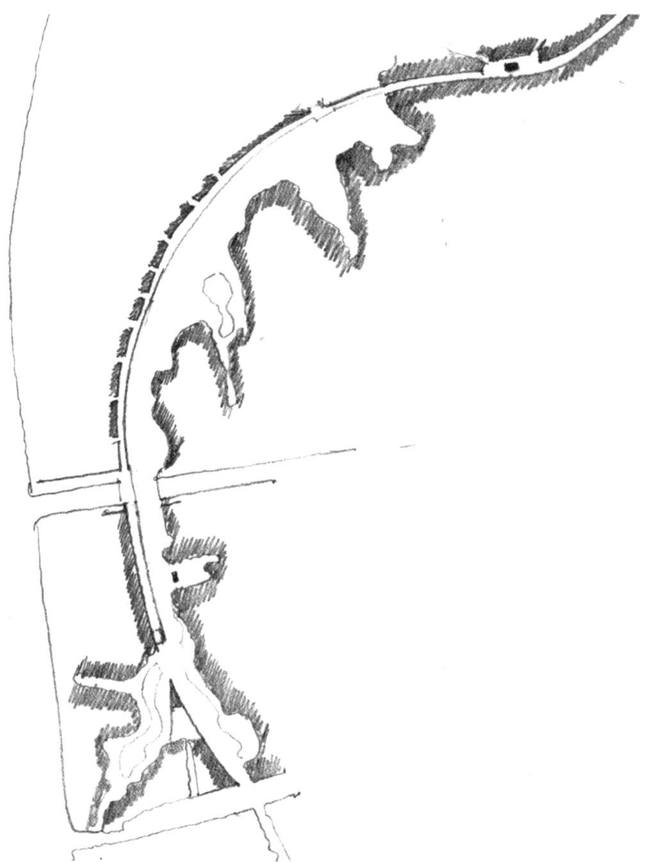

Figure 15

the Nazis shot almost 35,000 Jewish men, women, and children in cold blood. (Fig 11). As the Russian Army advanced to Kyiv, in their retreat, the Nazis forced Russian P.O.W. to fill in the ravine to conceal their crime. (Fig 12). Later, under the guise of progress, the Soviets built a formal park, cut the site with highways, and polluted it with toxic waste. In 1954, a large TV station was built on the historic Jewish Cemetery, and in 2000, the Metro was extended through the heart of the crime scene. The ravine lies concealed under multiple layers of desecration and denial. (Fig.12)

In 2016, on the 75th anniversary, the Ukrainian Jewish Encounter convened an international design competition with stringent constraints: only landscape, no structures, no memorials could be relocated, and no explicit Jewish religious symbols.

The topography of the ravine is the most significant clue missing to convey the mass graves and the magnitude of the terror. As a Jewish sacred site, Halakah law forbids any excavations of burial sites.

We created a pentimento with the 1943 Nazi aerial photograph onto the current topography as a diagnostic procedure to reveal the traces of the old ravine. (Fig 13) The pentimento gave us a template to repair the site's lost boundaries, and a new arc along the western edge links the Soviet Monument (1962) and the Menorah (1991). (Fig 14) Like a Kintsugi, we recovered the remaining fragment by gently clearing invasive trees. (Fig 15).

To honor the dead, the killing fields are transformed into a field of Yahrtzeit Candles. *Yahrzeit* is a Jewish mourning ritual; it marks a time to pray and remember (*Yizkor*) our lost loved ones. The different heights of LED lights in a moss garden evoke the lost topography. (Fig 15, 16).

The landscape becomes a memorial site, telling its story in a new way. Future visitors to the site will link these clues to imagine the crime scene and learn.

Pentimento is a metaphor that refers to the physical layers in the painting, and we extend it to the natural and settlement layers in the site. Pentimento, from Italian, *pentirsi*, means repentance, penance, regret.

Metanoia, or repentance, is that moment of grace when the truth about ourselves and God strikes us, pierces the heart, and makes new life possible. (Irénée Hausherr, SJ).

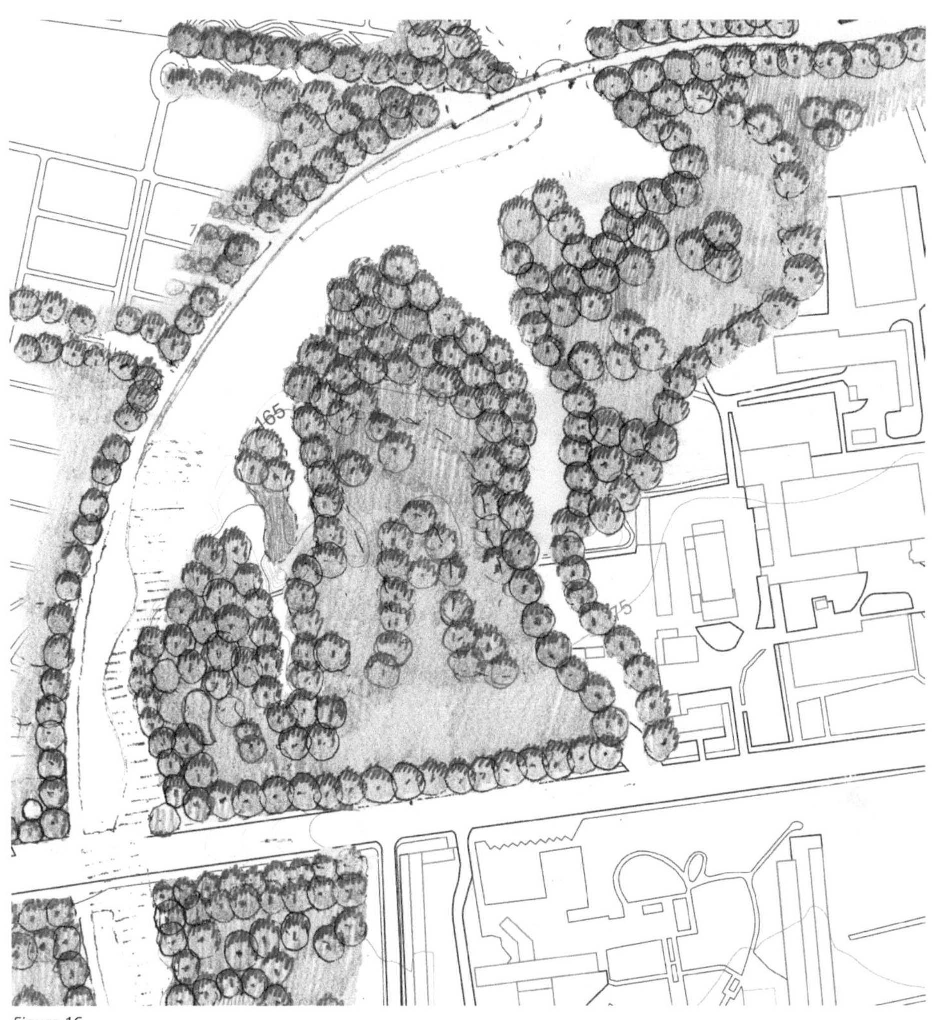

Figure 16

We may draw a distinction between guilt and repentance. Guilt is self-hatred; it depletes and defeats us. It brings depression and despair. Repentance recognizes and accepts pain and suffering. It is a state of recognition, the awareness of suffering and pain we may have caused. Repentance is a necessary step toward forgiveness and reconciliation. It can bring relief and freedom to let go of the past with resolve not to repeat our errors. Repentance is painful, yet it can be generous in spirit; it allows us to forgive ourselves and others for nurturing hope.

In our design practice, we are inspired by Urban Pentimento; it invokes form and emotion, body and soul, at the environmental scale. We weave together repose to contemplate, pentimento to repent, and kintsugi to repair, heal, and remember.

Memories do not cure, yet they can heal. Remembrance is a step toward repentance and a path toward truth and reconciliation. Our knowledge may be transformed into empathy and compassion. Our sorrow transformed into soulfulness.

Creativity can bring transformation and renewal; through forgiveness, it heals and nurtures faith in the future. These civic actions bind people to places and affirm life and love.

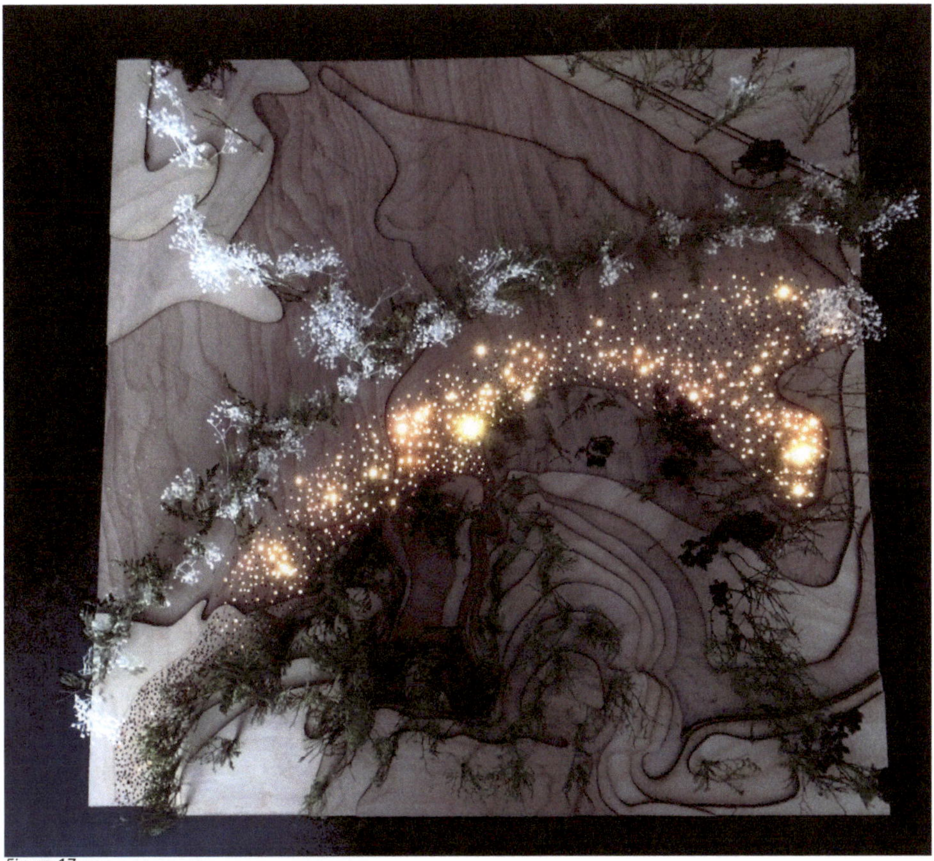

Figure 17

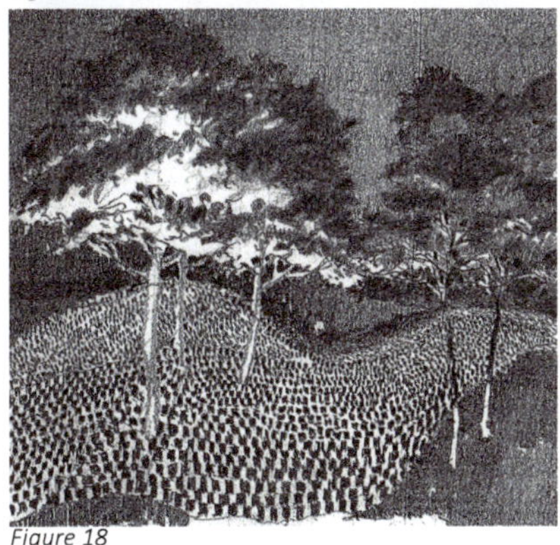

Figure 18

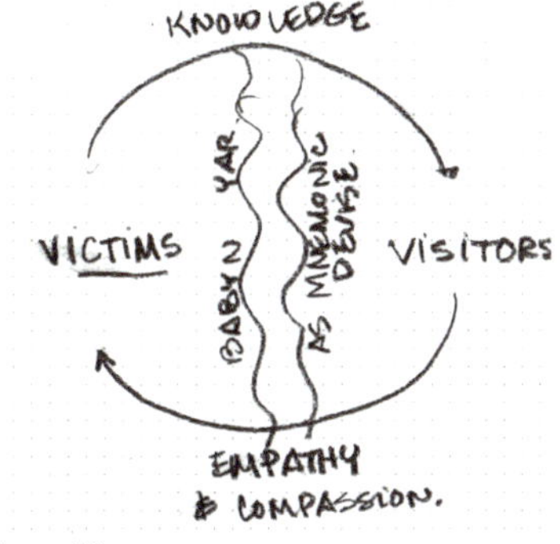

Figure 20

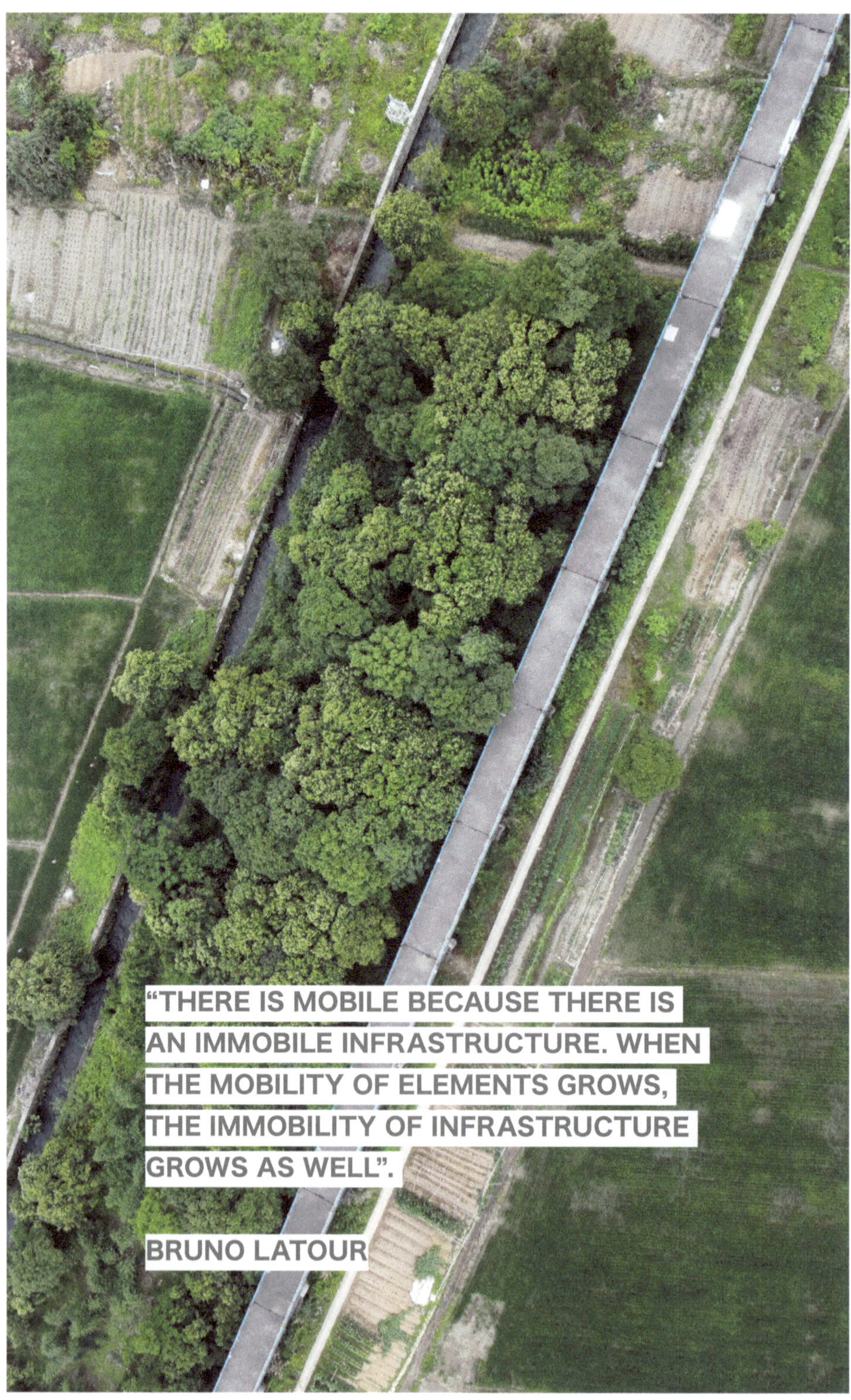

"THERE IS MOBILE BECAUSE THERE IS
AN IMMOBILE INFRASTRUCTURE. WHEN
THE MOBILITY OF ELEMENTS GROWS,
THE IMMOBILITY OF INFRASTRUCTURE
GROWS AS WELL".
BRUNO LATOUR

VINCENT PEU DUVALLON

PLUG-IN BRIDGE

FROM HERMES TO HESTIA

Movement and speed have fascinated architects at the end of the 20th century, from the writing of the philosopher Virilio to the theoretical work of the architect Bernard Tschumi. Movement and mobility have also been at the heart of urban and architectural discourse. The fascination for infrastructural landscapes is an attempt to integrate the immobility of buildings into the fluidity of networks.

This proposal for the valley of Caocun, in the south of China, inverts Tschumi's proposal and transforms the infrastructure, a vessel for mobility, into a series of public and resting spaces. The architecture happens when movement stops and rest begins.

The bridge crosses the valley, giving it scale. It is not the locus of Hermes, the god's messenger and symbol of travel, speed, and communication, but it becomes the place for Hestia, the goddess of the hearth, the domestic, one might say, the repose.

From means of transportation, they transform infrastructure into a supporting element for local activities—a place to link the visitors to the landscape—through platforms of observations.

The bridge is relatively narrow (three meters). A series of discrete modules are "plugged" into it to provide:

- Access to the bridges.
- Large-scale usages on the ground (swimming pool, library, restaurants).
- Small scale resting areas at the bridge height (sitting, lying, resting).

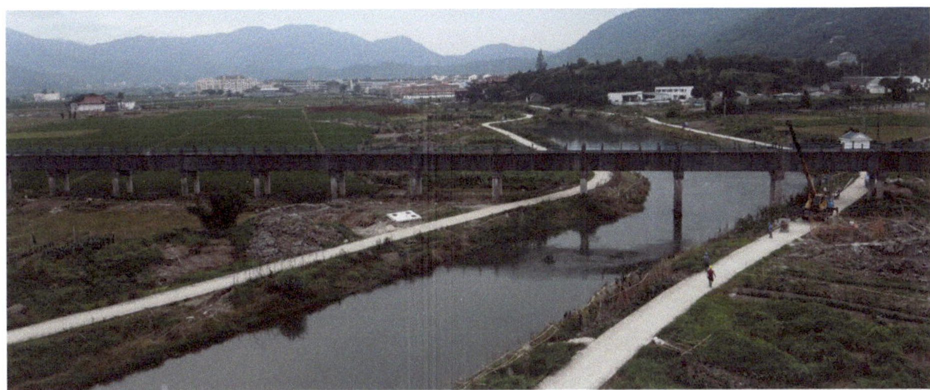

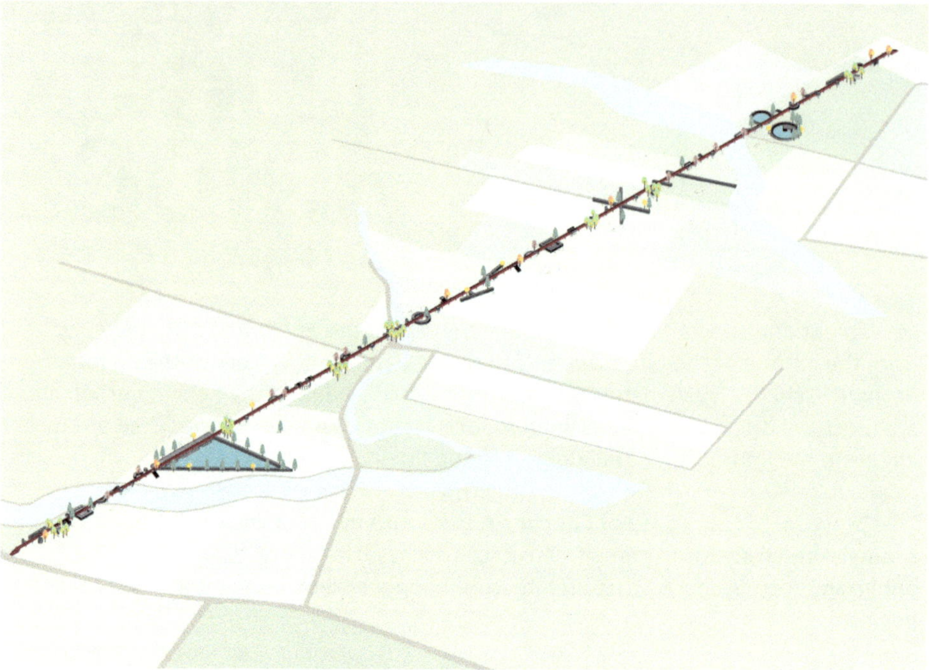

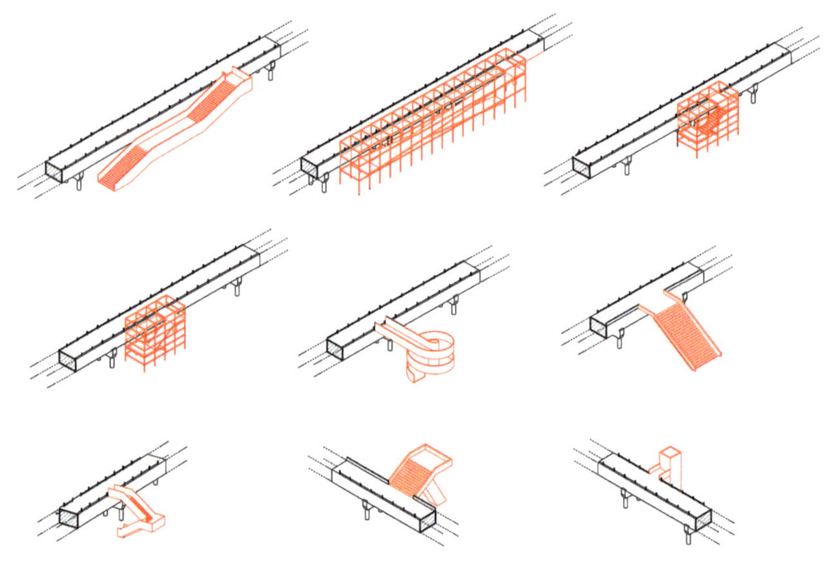

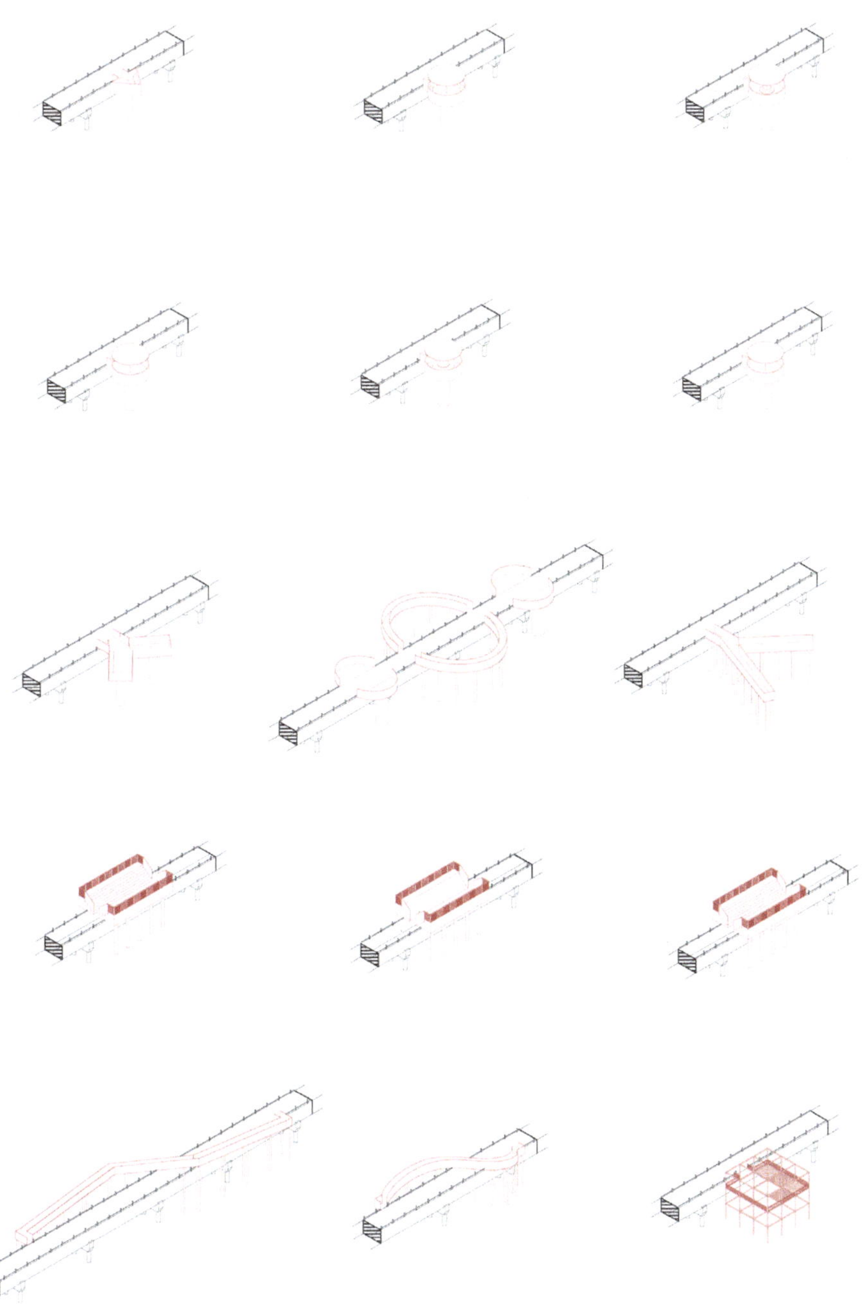

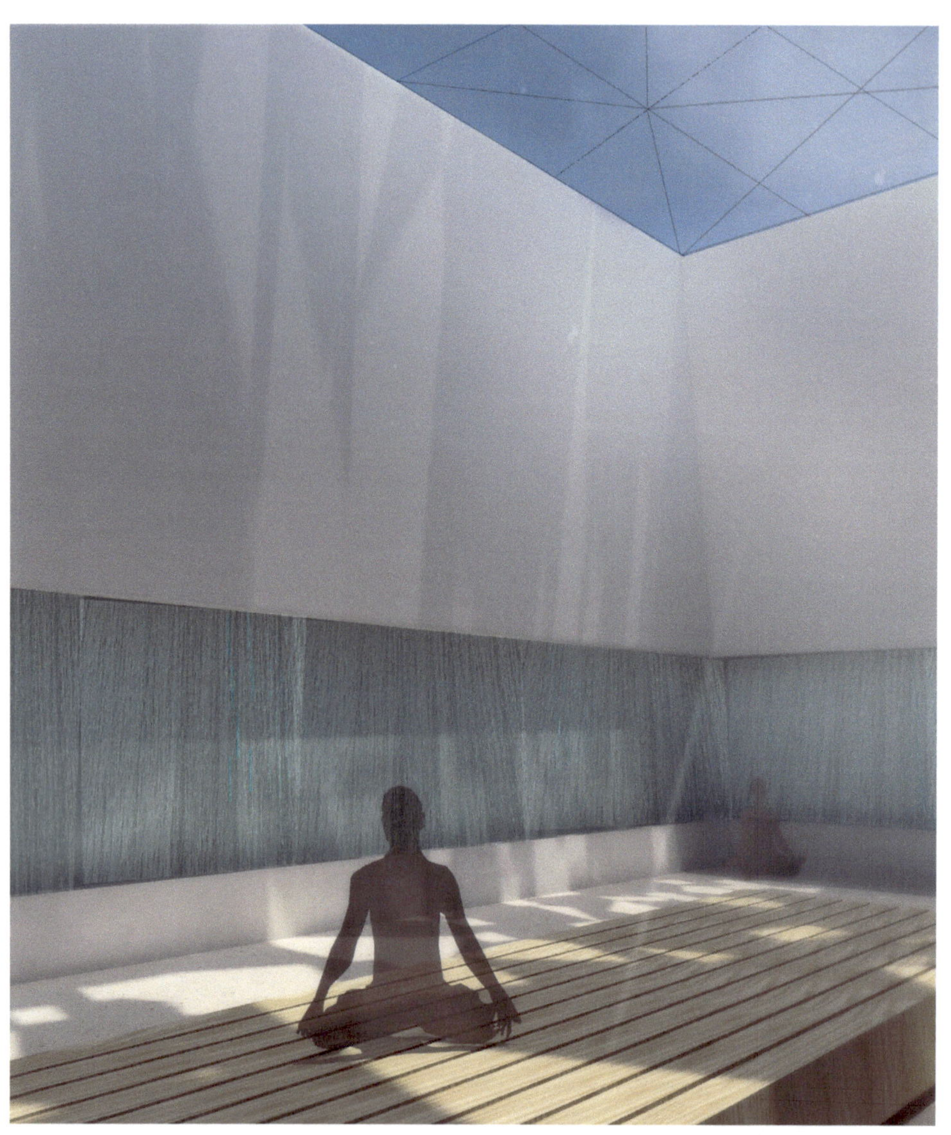

How to redefine sacred spaces, places of repose, for students of different cultures, ethnicities, and faiths on an dense urban campus?

KHASHAYAR SHAHKOLAHY

A PLACE FOR PEACE

TAMING AN URBAN MÉLANGE

The changing role of religion on campuses is documented in Margaret M. Grubiak,'s book, White Elephants on Campus: The Decline of the University Chapel in America, 1920–1960. Grubiak's convincing examples document the evolution of the architecture of recently constructed churches and chapels campuses shed light on religion's place, or lack therof, within tthe modern American university.

Architect, Shahkolahy, saw this unfulfilled need for students and faculty who live, work, and study in an academic environment embedded in the city of Baltimore. And he asked, where can one who is not connected to religion go within the clamor and commotion to find repose, solace, spiritual reflection? His search led him to a site convenient to the University of Baltimore and MICA (The Maryland Institute College of Art).

The site presented significant challenges and opportunities sitting at the confluence of multiple systems of transportation and urban support systems, including a waterway, railway, elevated highway, elevated roadway, parking lots, power distribution center, and city sewer systems pathway.

How then does Shahkolahy find solace within this whirlwind of motion systems? He proposes not a singular space or mandala but another system of movement—one allowing each visitor to find peace in their journey not through but around, above, and below the center.

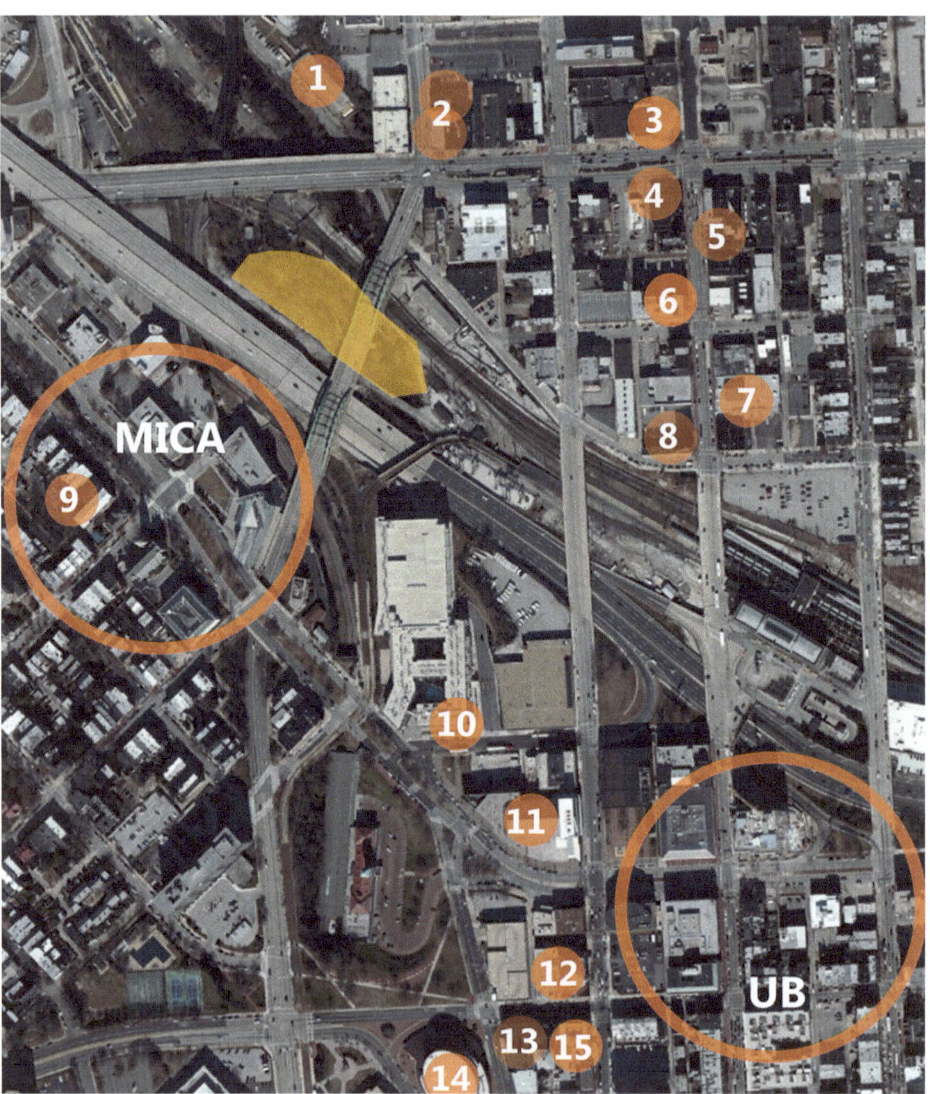

1. Streetcar Museum
2.Graffiti Warehouse- Load of Fun Arts
3 The Windup Space
4.Library and Info shop
5.Strand Theatre Company
6. Station North Art
7. The Charles Theatre
8. Metro Gallery
9. Corpus Chrisiti Church
10. Barnes and Nobles
11.Lyric Opera House
12. Greek Orthodox Church
13. Baltimore Theatre Project
14.Symphony Hall
15.Preston Hall

Site

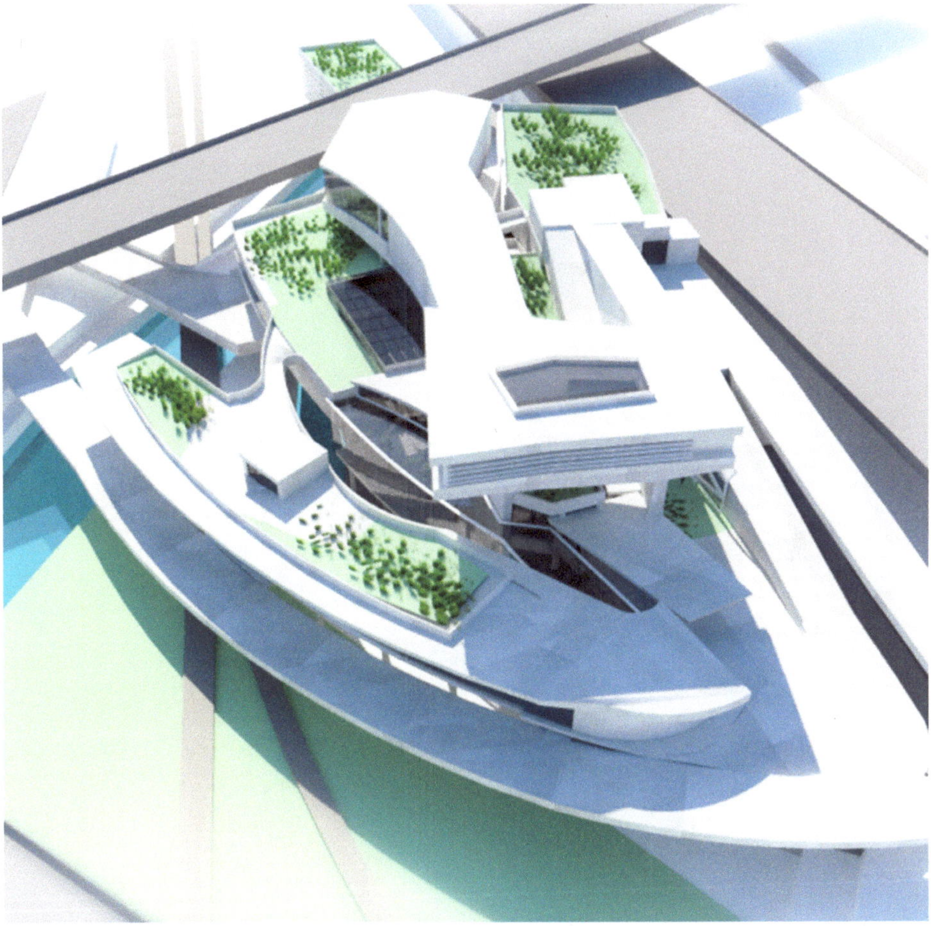

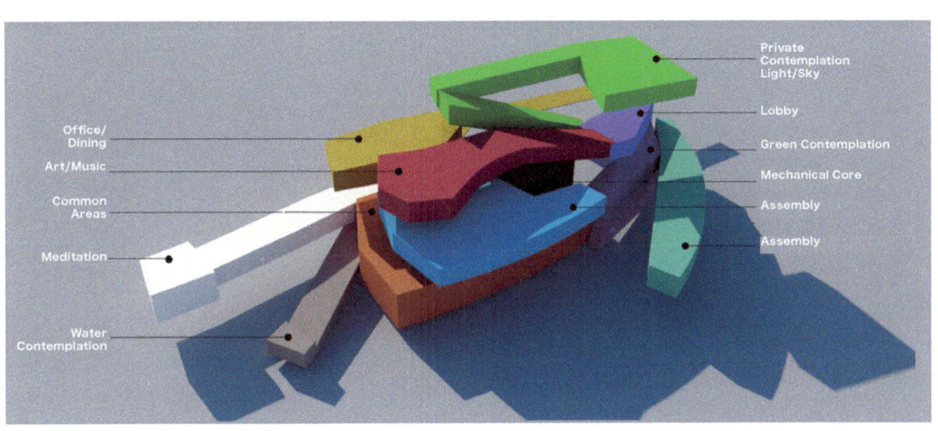
Private
Contemplation
Light/Sky
Lobby
Green Contemplation
Mechanical Core
Assembly
Assembly
Office/
Dining
Art/Music
Common
Areas
Meditation
Water
Contemplation

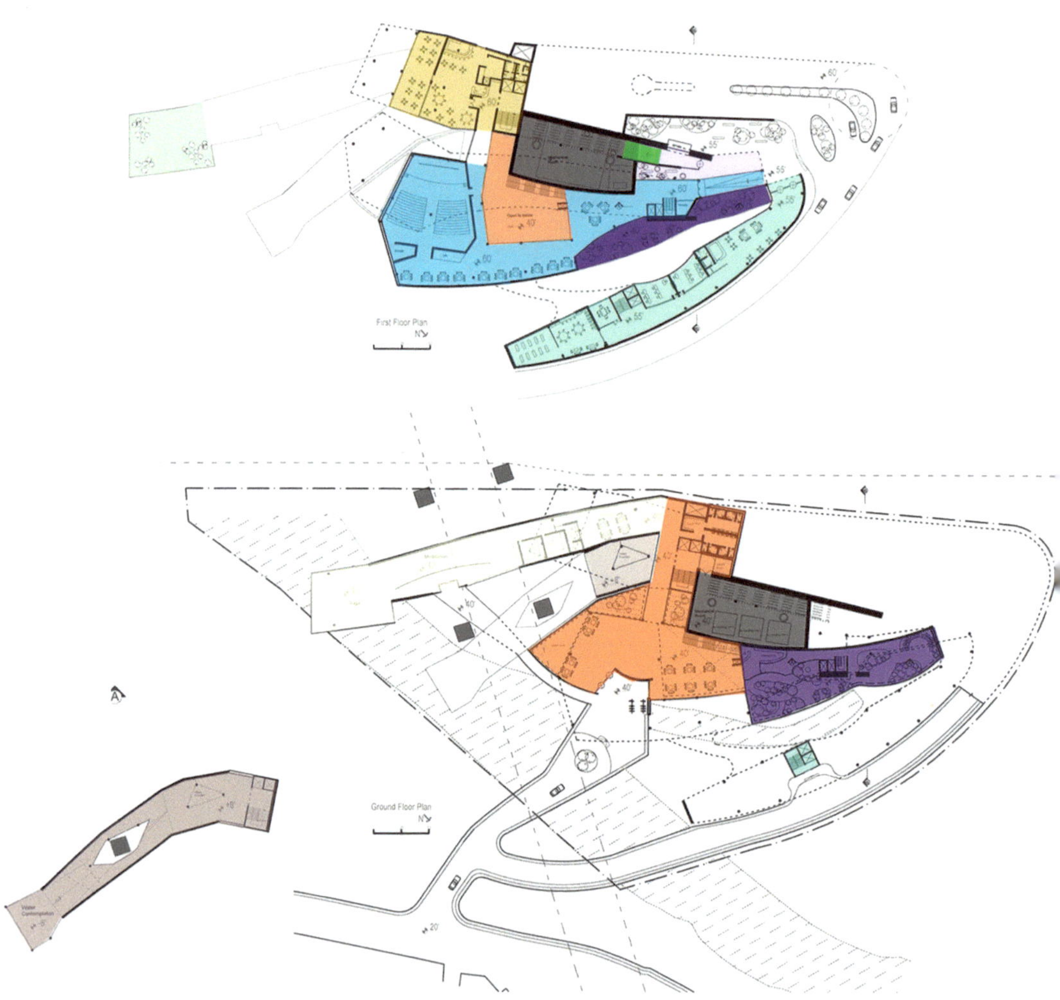
First Floor Plan
N
Ground Floor Plan
N

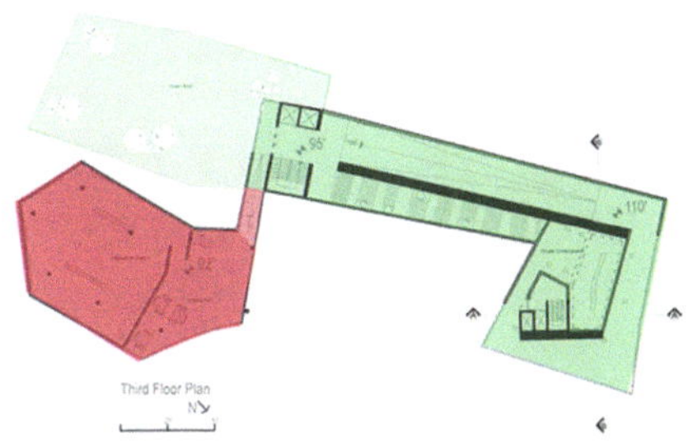
Third Floor Plan

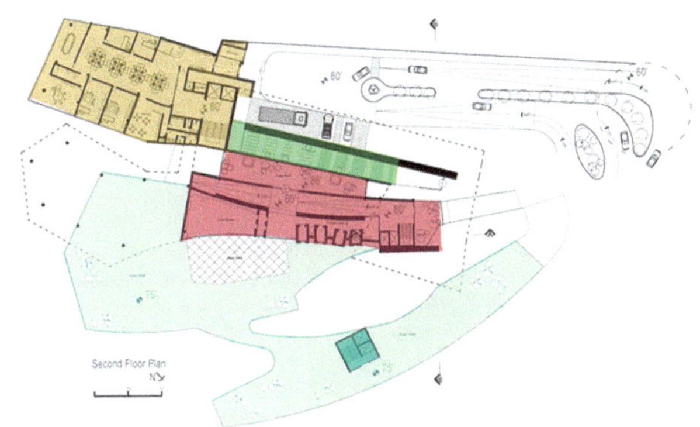
Second Floor Plan

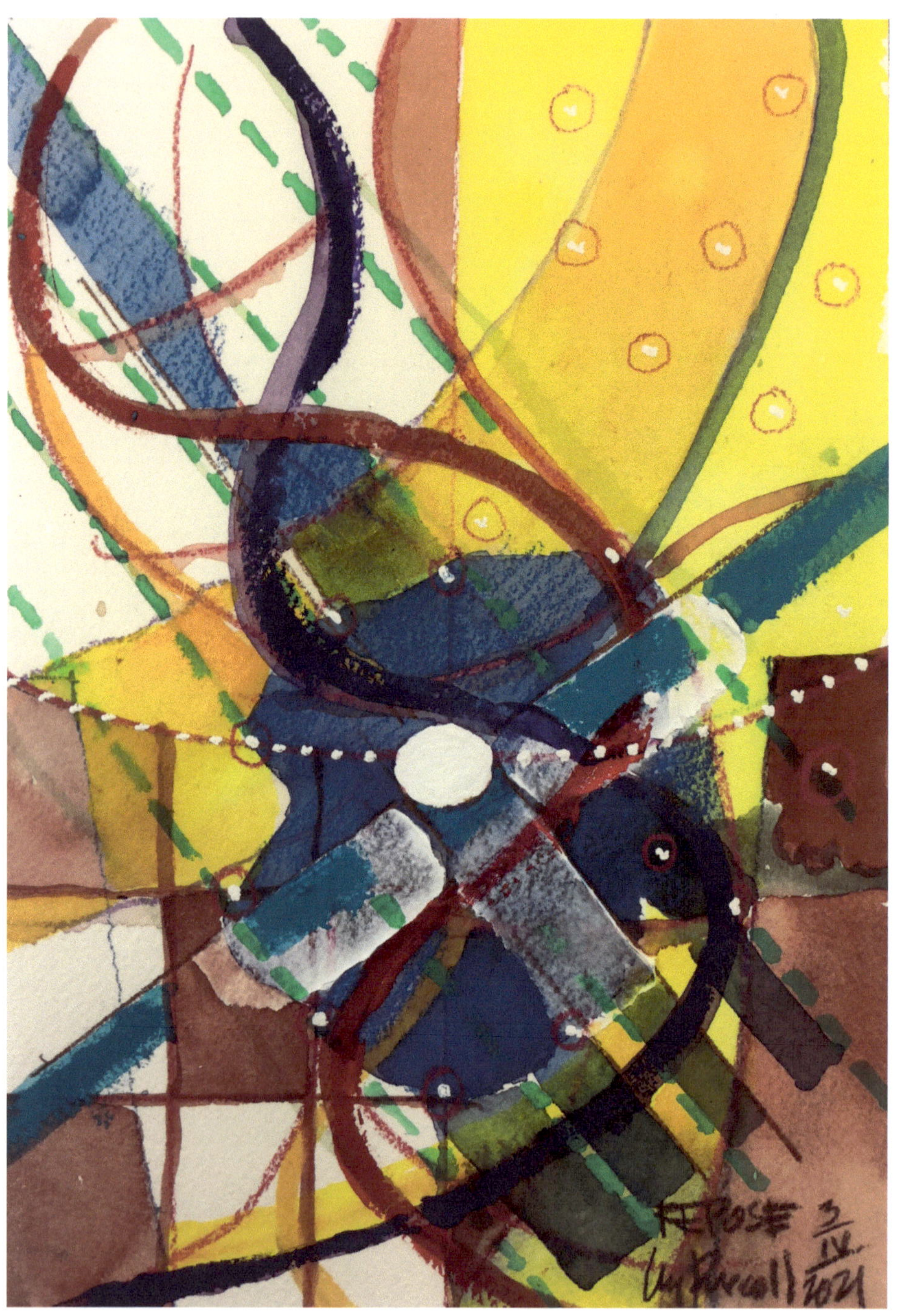

CRAIG PURCELL

[RE]POSE

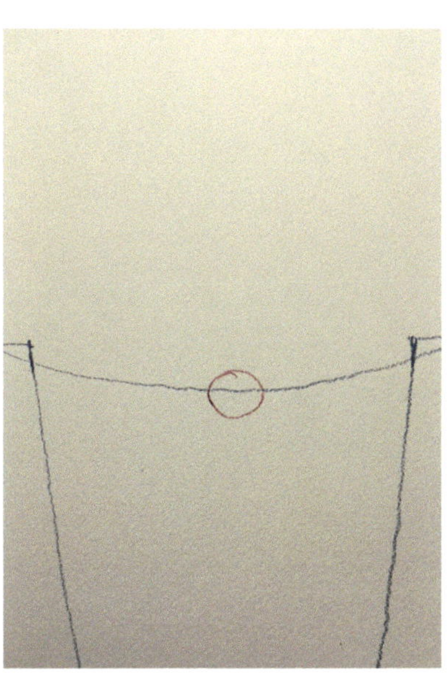

A guideline is a framework for Repose as it sails through time and space in a pitch, yaw, and roll fashion all the while changing state depending upon which field it encounters as web of resistance.

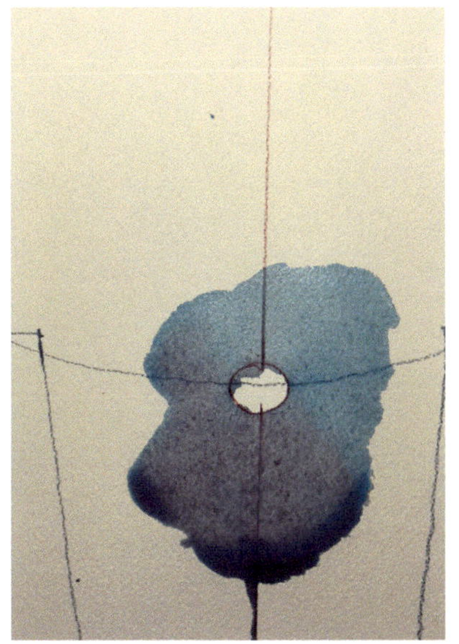

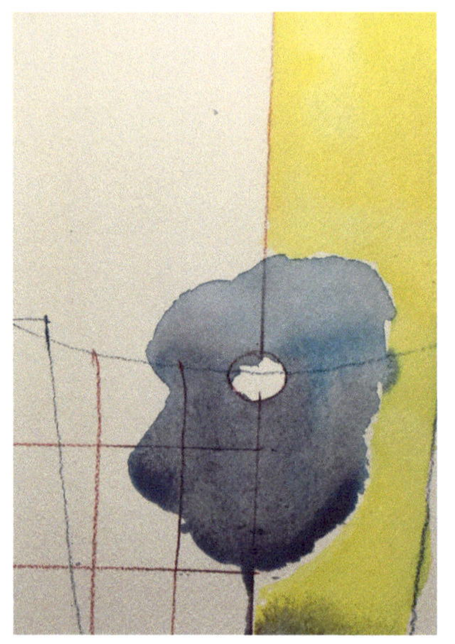

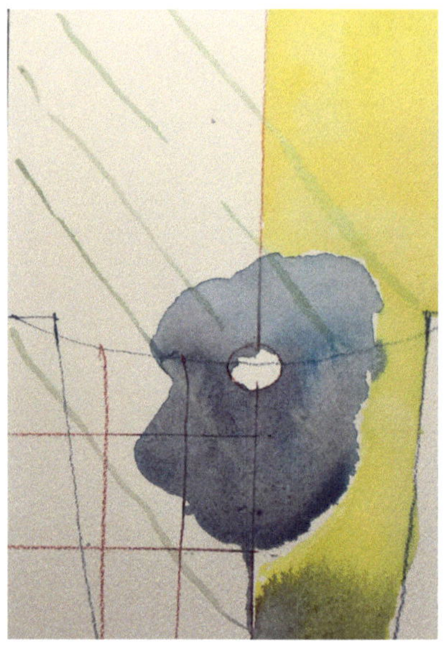

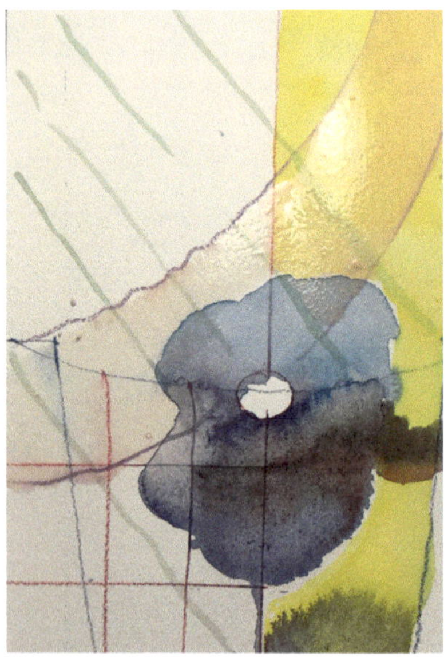

To be still in an
infinite continuum
is a challenge
and problematic
as all moves and
dances in a most
barycentric way
if only for for an
instant or for a cycle
or a century or
more.

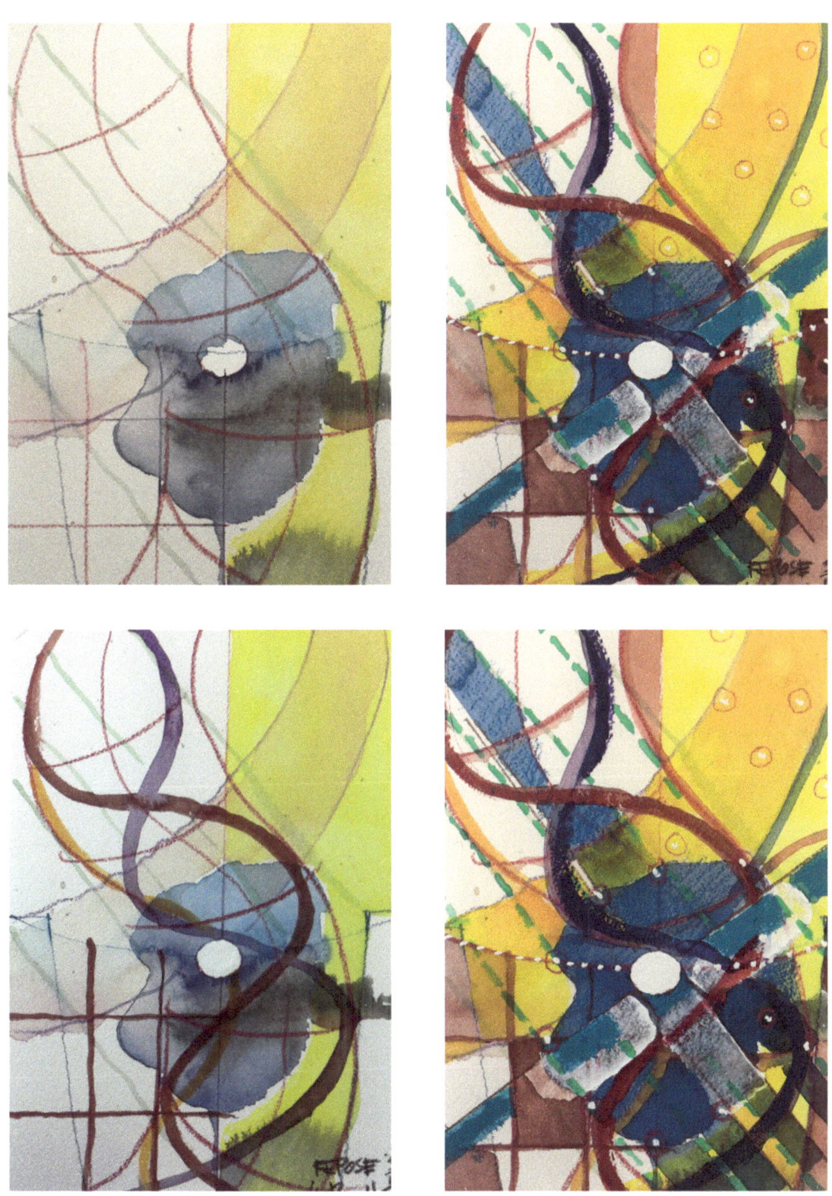

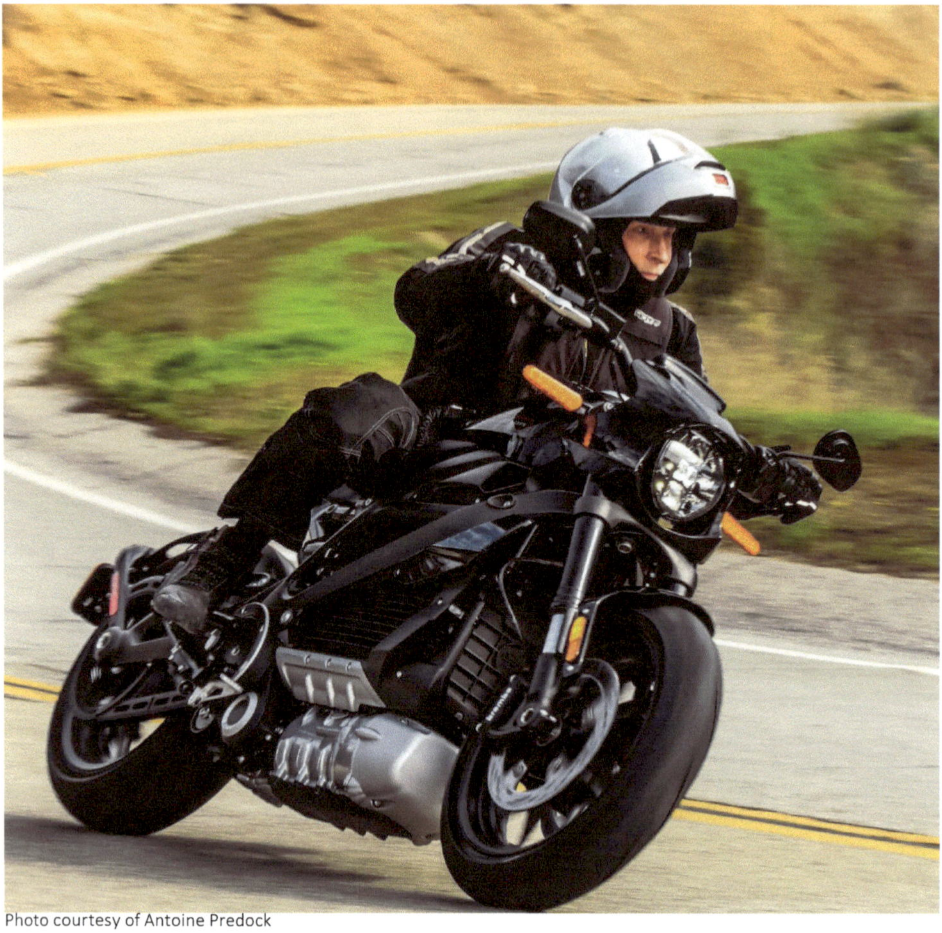

Photo courtesy of Antoine Predock

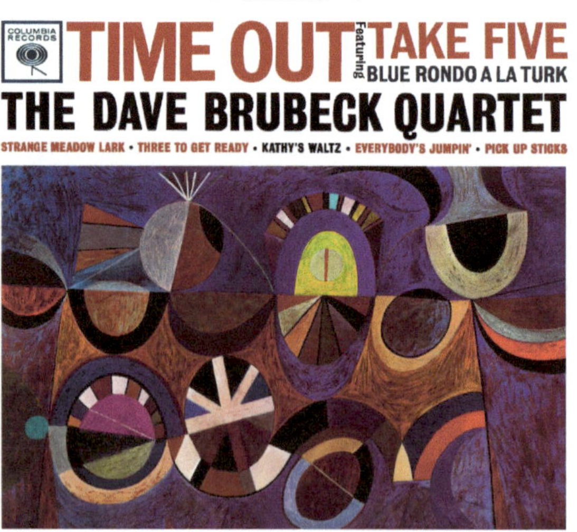

TAKING FIVE WITH ANTOINE PREDOCK

"Architecture is a fascinating journey toward the unexpected."

Although he is a man in constant motion, one can find repose in the work of Antoine Predock. From the contemplative spaces of the Canadian Museum for Human Rights to the serene desert landscapes that surround them, Predock's buildings provide a sense of peace and stillness in an often chaotic world. It is this careful balance of movement and stillness that makes his work so unique and compelling.

A Sense of Movement

Predock's buildings are often associated with movement and energy. The radial plan of the Canadian Museum for Human Rights, for example, encourages visitors to move through the space in a spiral pattern that gradually leads them upwards. This deliberate movement through the space mirrors the journey of self-discovery and reflection that museum-goers should experience as they learn about human rights violations throughout history.

In contrast, a series of sweeping curves that give it a sense of forward momentum characterizes the El Paso International Airport Terminal. This is appropriate for an airport, which is a place where people are constantly coming and going. The building's curved form also helps it blend in with the surrounding desert landscape, making it appear as though it has always been there.

A Sense of Repose

Besides movement, Predock's buildings also exhibit a great deal of repose. The Canadian Museum for Human Rights is situated atop a hill in Winnipeg's historic Forks district, providing visitors with stunning views of the cityscape below. The museum's glass façade also allows natural light to flood into the space, creating a tranquil and uplifting environment.

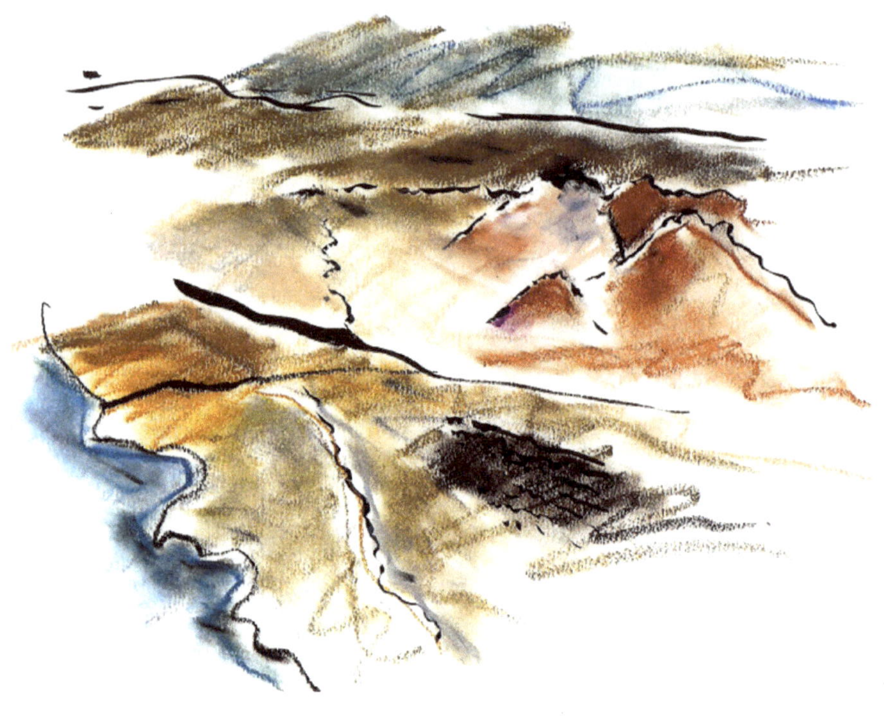

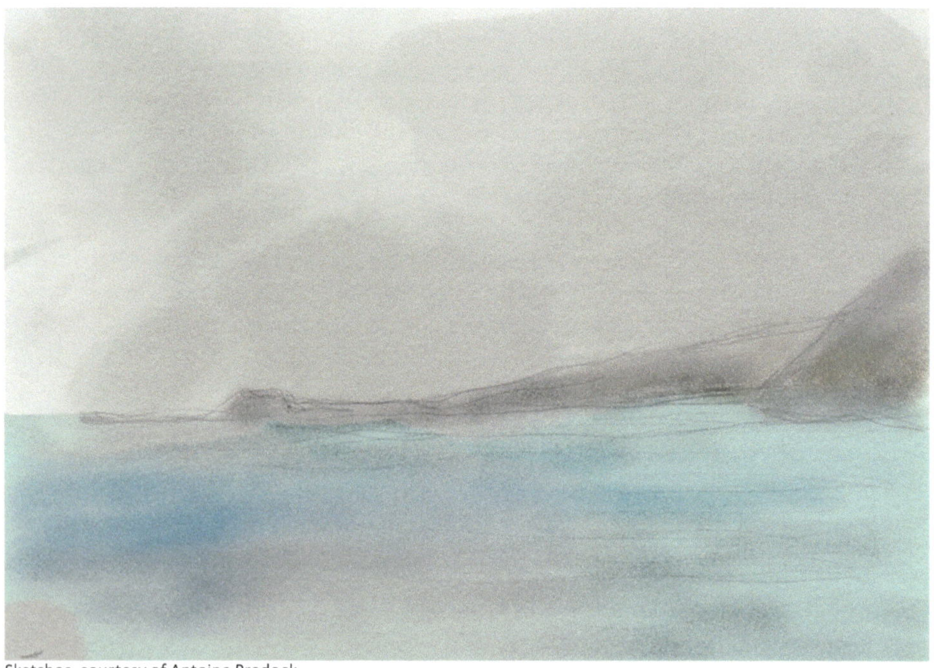

Sketches courtesy of Antoine Predock

The El Paso International Airport Terminal also takes advantage of its desert setting, with large windows that provide panoramic views of the landscape beyond. The material palette used throughout the terminal- including earth tones, wood, and stone- further ties it to its surroundings and gives it a calming atmosphere.

The Desert Landscapes: Spaces of Serenity

In contrast to the bustle of campus life, Arizona's desert landscapes provide a sense of serenity and stillness. These landscapes have served as inspiration for many of Predock's projects, including several residences he has designed in Scottsdale (a city in Greater Phoenix).

Their strong connection characterizes these residences to the desert landscape. Sometimes, this connection is literal—the house appears to emerge from the rocks and cacti that surround it. In other cases, it is more metaphorical—the home's design takes its cues from natural elements like sunlight and shadow.

Predock's architecture displays a reposeful quality that is informed by his experience with dance and the human body. Predock first gained exposure to the work of dancers and choreographers like Jennifer Masley, Merce Cunningham, and Yvonne Rainer while studying at the University of New Mexico. These artists emphasized spatial awareness and bodily control, which had a profound impact on Predock's understanding of architectural forms. Later, when he began working with dancer Anna Halprin, Predock further developed his interest in using architectural forms to express movement.

One can see the reposeful quality in his landscape sketches and his buildings resulting from these early influences. While the rhythms of dance clearly influenced his work, the influence of jazz musician Dave Brubeck is apparent. The angular forms of Predock's buildings and sketches express the irregular rhythms of Brubeck's music, suggesting that both artists were interested in creating a sense of dynamism through deliberate manipulation of traditional forms.

Editors:

Randy M. Sovich, FAIA, Editor

Randy Sovich holds a BArch from Carnegie-Mellon, and for the past 28 years has practiced as principal/founder of RM Sovich Architecture in Baltimore. His firm's work has been recognized with awards for innovative housing, healthcare, adaptive reuse, and design for aging. His project, with Peter Fillat, "New Urban Housing" received a Progressive Architecture Award. He was elected to the AIA College of Fellows in 2022.

Lynda Burke, Co-Editor

Lynda Burke graduated from Georgetown University with a Bachelor of Science in Languages and Linguistics and has done substantial graduate work in the field of Comparative Literature. She has diverse professional experience, currently working as a free-lance editor and translator

Craig N. Purcell, Co-Editor

An architect with over 35 years of experience, Purcell is devoted to the study of the architecture and physical organization of cities. He earned his BS Arch at the University of Virginia. His Urban Design team won Most Resilient Design in AIA Baltimore's Resilient: Rowhouse Competition 2015.

Advisors:

David Seamon is an environment-behavior researcher and Professor of Architecture at Kansas State University in Manhattan, Kansas. His research and writings focus on the ways that the natural and built environments contribute to human wellbeing.

Kent C. Bloomer has over fifty years of experience as an exhibiting sculptor, practicing designer, and professor. Bloomer earned a BFA is physics and architecture at Massachusetts Institute of Technology. He studied sculpture at Yale University, and earned his MFA in 1961. Bloomer's sculpture has been exhibited by numerous museums and galleries, including the Museum of Modern Art in New York City. He is the author of Body, Memory and Architecture and The Nature of Ornament, among others, and has taught architectural ornament at Yale University for over forty years.

Contributors

Alan Paige Lightman

Alan Paige Lightman is an American physicist, writer, and social entrepreneur. He has served on Harvard University and Massachusetts Institute of Technology (MIT) faculties. Currently a Professor of the Practice of the Humanities at the Massachusetts Institute of Technology (MIT), Lightman played a significant role in establishing MIT's "Communication Requirement," which requires all undergraduates to have training in writing and speaking each of their four years. Lightman was one of the first people at MIT to have a joint faculty position in both the sciences and the humanities. In his thinking and writing, Lightman is known for exploring the intersection of the sciences and the humanities, especially the dialogue between science, philosophy, religion, and spirituality.

Ioana Barac

Ioana Barac is a designer, maker, and educator whose practice straddles the fields of art and architecture. She is partner and co-founder of Atelier Cue, a place-making, community engagement and public art studio in New Haven, CT. From object to city-scale, the studio's work incorporates rhythm, light and narrative elements, and evolves through collaborative processes that connect communities with their public places and with each other. Ioana studied architecture and urbanism in Romania and in the U.S. and is a graduate of Yale University and of University of Hartford, where she teaches architectural, urban and ornament design. Ioana has extensive experience in the creation of architectural ornament and place-based art and believes in their power to bridge the local and the universal.

Beniamino Servino

Beniamino Servino was born in St. Joseph in Vesuvius, Italy. He graduated in 1985 from the Faculty of Architecture Federico II in Naples. In 1994 Servino initiated Serven, a think tank built around the question of the monumental in architecture and in the context of a post-ecological city-territory. More recently, he defined and updated a manual of the Aesthetics of Misery Dignified. His architecture, drawings, and montages are widely published, including CASA MALAPARTE. Re-writing of an untouchable text. As an act of love (2015), OBVIUS a theory of architecture in the form of a diary (2014), MONUMENTAL NEED (2012), and ARCHITECTURA SIMPLEX (2012).

Nicole Cullinan

Nicole has an established career in the architecture and arts industry in content creation, photography, and writing. She is a visual art contributor for *Beyond Words* Literary magazine and had a photo exhibited in *Photo 2021*, collaborating with French artist JR at Federation Square. She was also Highly Commended in the *Mono Photography Competition* in 2021. Nicole is currently undertaking a research project and believes the architect's work can be more than what the eye can see; *'allegoria dei sensi,'* A trinity of function, form and feeling.

Miriam Gusevich

Miriam is a Cuban - American urban designer, scholar, and teacher. She is the founding principal at GM2 Studio and a professor at CUA in Washington, DC. An experienced city maker, her work is inspired by the story of each site to reconcile and guide publicaction. Recent international awards include "Zenica Kilim," Bosnia (2019), and two memorial masterplans in Ukraine: "Constellations" for Euro-Maidan (2015) and "Yahrzeit Candles" for Babyn-Yar (2016). "Sambir" and "Ralivka" are two current commissions for Holocaust landscapes near Lviv. Other highlights are the Jane Addams Memorial Park with Louise Bourgeois, Cancer Survivor's Park, Mandrake Park, all in Chicago, and the People's Plan for McMillan Park, in Washington, DC. Miriam also has a distinguished academic career with a long list of lectures, publications, and grants. She received her M.Arch'79 and B.Arch'75 from Cornell University and was a Loeb Fellow'97 at Harvard University.

Vincent Peu Duvallon

Vincent Peu Duvallon is the co-founder and the lead designer for architecture and interior design of oncestudio, an architecture and design office based in Wenzhou, China. Beside his practice he is also assistant professor and the executive director of the School of Public Architecture at Michael Graves College in Wenzhou-Kean University.

Khashayar Shashkolay, AIA

A licensed architect in New York state, Khashayar Koly earned his Master's in Structural Engineering from Columbia University in 2021, his MArch from Morgan State in 2015, and his undergraduate degree from Shiraz University, Iran, in 2008. His professional experience includes projects in public transportation, justice, and healthcare. Throughout his education and experience, Khash believes structure and architecture should integrate at all steps of a project; the architect/structural engineer relationship is essential in delivering a successful project.

Joseph Mullan

Joseph Mullan taught photography at Wesley College and is a commercial photographer in Wilmington DE. Mullan's photography was awarded first place in the Landscape Category of the 2013 Spirit of Place 40th Anniversary Photo and Video Contest; his still photograph won the top award in the 2011 Precision Image Competition. Mullan received his MFA from Maine Media College.

Janet Little Jeffers

Janet Little Jeffers is a Baltimore, Maryland-based artist specializing in digital photography. After working in graphic design, interior design, and broadcasting, she committed to a full-time career as a visual artist in 2009. Her work explores intimate and abstract details in the natural and artificial worlds, and she thrives on exploration in her hometown or a remote destination. Some of her recent projects include bodies of work from Cuba and the polar regions of Greenland and Antarctica.

The Editors would like to thank Edward S. Casey for his support and encouragement.

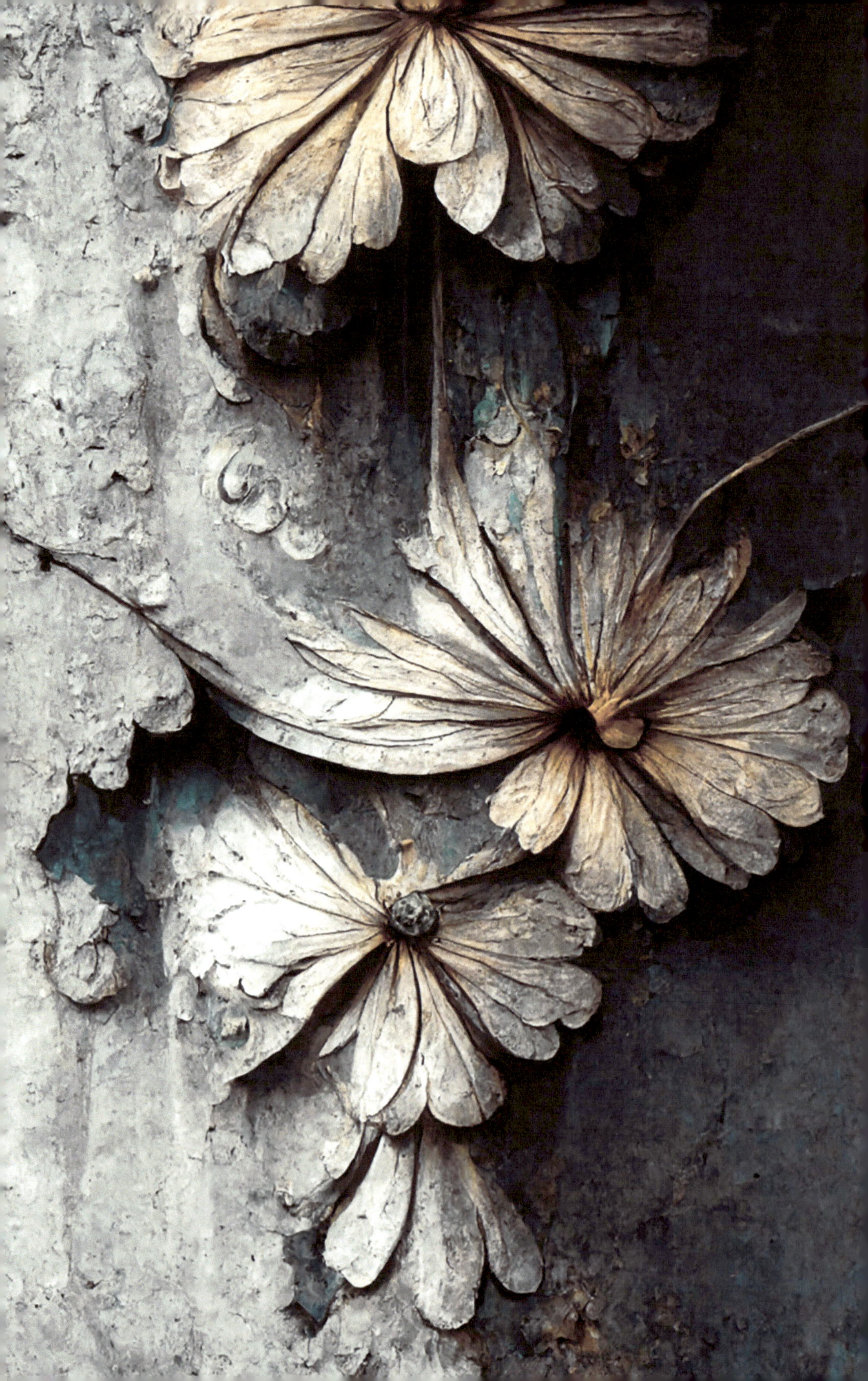

www.ingramcontent.com/pod-product-compliance
Lightning Source LLC
LaVergne TN
LVHW052308100826
845147LV00006B/699